SUPPER
with Love

SUPPER
with Love

Vibrant, Delicious, and Comforting Plant-Forward
and Pescatarian Recipes for Every Day

Michelle Braxton

PHOTOGRAPHY BY ERIN SCOTT

HARVEST
An Imprint of WILLIAM MORROW

Contents

WITH LOVE AND *Gratitude*

If it wasn't for the people who helped me turn what was once only a vision dancing around in my head into a reality, *Supper with Love* would not exist, and for them I'm forever grateful. So, before we dig in and eat . . . with love and gratitude.

ALEX—From our first slow dance in high school to now. Look at how far we've come. My love, none of this would have been possible without your love, support, patience, and endless encouragement. The last couple of years were centered around this book and it was a tremendous sacrifice, with so many late nights, early mornings, and long days and weekends, but even still you pushed me to strive for more. Thank you . . . thank you . . . thank you! Infinite LOVE, always.

MY *SUPPER WITH MICHELLE* FAMILY—This book has been a long time coming. You all are what have made this journey amazing. YOU are my people. YOU are my village. Thank you for visiting the blog and sharing with me . . . all the dishes that you've made your own. For sending me emails or DMs, and stopping me randomly on the street. I've truly enjoyed engaging with and getting to know so many of you over the years, and I look forward to seeing this book in all of your hands and all of the dishes that you will create, so be sure to tag me and share them with me!

MICHELLE—Girl, whew! I can't even write this without crying. Pass me a tissue! Haha! My sister from my other mother, thank you for always being so supportive and honest, for always telling me all of the things I needed to hear and the things that I didn't want to hear, but needed to. Love you girl and you, too, Monique, Jada, Jason, and Joey!

SHARON—Thank you for being a second "mother" to me and a friend. For welcoming me into your family. And for supporting me and being a cheerleader for *Supper with Michelle*. Love you!

ABDESLAM—Thank you for being Mom's everything and for loving her and making her incredibly happy. Love you!

MY FAMILY—Andrea, Nicole, Yvonne (and all of my nieces and nephews), Uncle Bebe and Auntie Gayle, all of my cousins and the rest of the Braxton crew. I hope that I've made you proud. To the entire Conley and Anderson family (Stephanie, Anthony, Sean, Melissa, Damon, Monaiy, Damarion) . . . love y'all!

MY EXTENDED FAMILY AND FRIENDS—Brenda (DaiQuann, BriAun, Robierra), Kelly and the Lipscomb family, the Cain family, Terra, Gudrun, Deborah and Rene, Jamila, Angelique, Nakita (Jalin), Malin, Karen, Toni, Shannon, Beth and Curtis, Luladae . . . love y'all!

MY NEIGHBORS—Barbara, Cynthia, Lester, Benita, Leroy, Chuck, Kia, Deborah, and Tony. Thank you for always being willing to take any container of food (and there were a lot!) that I sent your way and for providing me with your thoughts and feedback on all of the recipes I was testing.

DESTIN—Thank you for always being willing to try any and every dish I put before you with an open mind and open heart.

YOLANDA AND ZANA—Yolanda! THANK YOU! Aside from Alex and myself, I think you're the only other person who tasted almost every recipe in the book! Our conversations about each and your feedback was invaluable and I appreciate you so much. You and Zana have such an incredible way with words and in describing everything that you see and taste. It just meant so much and I thank you from the bottom of my heart. Zana! Thank you for being another set of eyes for me when my brain was almost completely fried.

LEIGH—Thank you for being such a dope literary agent and for sometimes holding my hand when I didn't know what the heck I was doing . . . and for having my back from start to finish with this project. Your knowledge and experience are indispensable and any author would truly be lucky to have you as their agent.

MY TEAM AT HARPER DESIGN—Soyolmaa Lkhagvadorj, thank you for loving and believing in my project from the very beginning. Jenna Lefkowitz, I appreciate everything you did to help bring this project together and for being my liaison through it all. Lynne Yeamans, thank you for being my go-to person and for fielding my one million questions during all of our Zoom meetings. Marta Schooler, thank you for ensuring the early stages of this book went seamlessly. Tricia Levi, thank you for your meticulous edits, for pushing me to dig deep, and for asking all the important questions. Dori Carlson and Stacey Fischkelta, thank you for making the copyediting stage painless.

MY TEAM AT HARVEST—Deb Brody, Stephanie Fletcher, and everyone else behind the scenes at Harvest. You all picked up the baton near the end of this project and kept this baby rolling without missing a beat. Jacqueline Quirk, thank you for being my go-to person, fielding all of my questions, making ALL of the things happen, and for all of your feedback.

LAURA PALESE—Thank you for your patience and for beautifully bringing my vision to life and making me incredibly proud to hold this book in my hands.

MY PHOTOGRAPHY DREAM TEAM—Y'all did the damn thing! What a trip, starting with us driving across the country from Atlanta, Georgia, to Berkeley, California! Words truly can't express how grateful I am to you all for helping bring my recipes to life. Erin Scott you are AMAZING! I can't thank you enough for pulling off all ten days of shooting. So many moving pieces, but you did it! Thank you for being patient with me and for going beyond to make me oh so happy and proud of the work we accomplished together. Lillian Kang, thank you for all of the crispy and crunchy bits, for your attention to detail, and your desire for perfection, including those baby basil leaves, all the drips, drizzles, and crumbs, and for nailing Mom's soup, which brought me to tears. Paige Arnett, I know I got on your nerves, but thanks for adding your love into each of these recipes and for letting me peek into your pots and get in your way in the kitchen! You rocked it! Tamer Abu-Dayyeh, thanks for lending a hand on my lifestyle day and our last day of shooting! Shawn Burke, you made me feel so at ease and made me look so natural. I wish you lived closer! Allison Fellion, Girlfriend! That was *a lot* of food you had to buy . . . so thank you.

INSPIRATIONAL CHEFS, AUTHORS, CREATORS, AND WRITERS IN THE FOOD AND BLOGGING COMMUNITY—Adrianna Guevara Adarme, Alanna Taylor-Tobin, Alexandra Stafford, Ali Maffucci, Allison Day, Amisha Gurbani, Amy Chaplin, Anela Malik, Asha Shivakumar, Ashlea Carver, Ashley Marti, Bryant Terry, Carina Wolff, Chitra Agrawal, Colu Henry, Dale Gray, Danielle Kartes, Deb Abbott, Deborah Balint, Diala Canelo, Diane Morrisey, Dimity Jones, Emilie Raffa, Emma Morris, Erika Council, Erin Alderson, Gayle Mcleod, Grace Elkus, Heidi Swanson, Jamie Vespa, Jeanine Donofrio, Jenné Claiborne, Jeri Mobley, Jerrelle Guy, Jessica Jones, Jessica Merchant, Jill Fergus, Jocelyn Delk Adams, Joy Wilson, Julia Turshen, Justine Doiron, Kayla Stewart, Klancy Miller, Kris Warman, Kristina Cho, Laura Miner, Laura Wright, Leigh Ann Chatagnier, Liren Baker, Marisa Moore, Michelle Arbus, Natasha Bull, Rebecca Firth, Rosalynn Daniels, Sara Forte, Sarah Britton, Shakayla Scott, Shanika Graham-White, Shauna Sever, Sheil Shukla, Shelly Westerhausen Worcel, Shira McDermott, Sonia Wong, Sonja Overhiser, Sophie MacKenzie, Tabitha Brown, Teri Turner, Traci York, Vallery Lomas, Virginia Willis, and Wendy Lopez, you all have helped or inspired me in some way over the years. Some through conversations, advice, or kind words, or for just being the beautiful and inspiring people that you are.

MY RECIPE TESTERS—Y'all showed up and showed out! I appreciate you all so much for working these recipes into your already busy lives. For providing so much valuable feedback on each and every recipe. You made me consider so many things I had not thought of and I'm grateful. Thank you Abby Stephenson, Amy Miller, Ann Vander Hijde, Annie Diamond, April Dembraski, Aynsley Morris, Barbara Fogel, Beverly Tidwell, Callie Rose, Carrie Chestnut, Carrie Johnson, Christine Ederer, Clare Langan, Courtney Spiegl, Crystal Ryu, Danita Day, Earth Johnson, Ellie VandenBerg, Emily Walsh, Erica Eliason, Erin Wagner, Jackie Kallberg, Jenna Dworkin, Jennifer Kennedy, Jennifer Speier, Jessica B. Harris, Johanna Dishongh, Julie Chappell, Katie Peterson, Katie Robinson, Kelli Foster, Kim Silva, Kricia Morris, Lisa Salko, Margaret French, Michelle Rogers, Neva Sypniewski, Renee Harris, Samantha Spiesman, Sara Verk, Shanna Bennett, Soula Pefkaros, Tesia Geyer, and Tina Albrecht.

CONTRIBUTING BRANDS—A special thank you to Zwilling J. A. Henckels (Meredith Bradford, you're the best and I love my cookware and small appliances!), New York Shuk (Leetal Arazi, I love your harissa!), and Pearls (I love your olives!).

FOR THOSE OF YOU who bought this book, were gifted this book, or checked it out from your local library . . . thank you. And to those who I may not have personally thanked, blame it on all of these silver strands on top of my head . . . and not my heart. Much love!

A JOURNEY OF FOOD,
Love, and Life

When my agent first approached me in 2021 and asked if I ever thought about writing a cookbook, I knew that I wanted to do it but there was one major factor that pushed me to agree. You see . . . when I was growing up, when I turned on the TV, no one looked like me on any of the cooking shows. And when I visited my local bookstore or library, there were only a small handful of Black people whose names, and sometimes images, graced the covers of cookbooks. It wasn't until adulthood that I started to see slow progress. Regardless, I felt it important to create the kind of book that I wished to see more of on book shelves across the world. And share a piece of my journey in hopes that it might inspire other people—home cooks, chefs, food bloggers, creatives, writers—to keep doing what they love and possibly find an avenue to share their stories as well. Our voices are all so beautifully unique and they deserve an opportunity and platform to be shared and heard.

As a first-time cookbook author, I had absolutely no idea what I was doing when I began writing *Supper with Love* in 2021. Like many of you, I'm just someone who truly loves to cook for the people I love or for anyone who needs a warm meal. However, I didn't realize how extremely difficult it would be to write this book. Not difficult in the sense that it was laborious. I mean, don't get me wrong, it was a labor of love. What I mean to say is that it was difficult emotionally. Writing this book was incredibly introspective, and because of that, I am certainly not the same woman now that I was going into it. It took a lot of courage to open up and to be in a slightly vulnerable state. This book evolved into something far more than just the recipes that fill it. It became part of my legacy—and a time capsule, if you will. As I developed and cooked each of these recipes, the sights, the tastes, and the smells evoked many forgotten memories, both joyous and sad, and elicited a few tears as well. The wonderful thing about food is not just its ability to fuel and nourish our bodies but its ability to bring us together—just as it has done with you and me.

When I was growing up, I think my mom would have preferred going out to dinner every night rather than cooking it. Although she enjoyed cooking—sometimes on the weekends, for special occasions, or during the holidays—she didn't enjoy doing it daily. She and my father divorced when I was really young, and she was just starting off in her career. Money was *extremely* tight, and she spent many nights working late hours, coming home completely exhausted. But all of her hard work eventually paid off, and she bought our first house. It was a small house in a close-knit neighborhood in Decatur, Georgia, just outside of Atlanta. And having a strong sense of community was always important to Mom, along with having neighbors that she knew and could depend on.

I was too young to comprehend it at the time, but I now understand part of the reason my journey with food began at such an early age. It was a necessity for me to be able to function in the kitchen. Mom was a single parent who had to work long hours, and she needed me to be more independent and start helping out around the house. When I turned seven, Mom slowly began to show me little things in the kitchen. I recall pulling my little yellow chair up to the stove to stand on as she showed me how to adjust the flame on our old gas range.

That was all it took to fuel my love for cooking. After that, I started to feel like Julia Child (who we would watch a lot during that time), and I was eager for her to show me more.

The meals I made when I was young weren't always home-cooked, per se. They were simple things like frozen TV dinners, pot pies, Stouffer's meals, Campbell's soups, and many other foods that came from a can or box (and were often eaten on a TV tray in front of the TV). Gradually I ventured into other things like baked potatoes, salads, sandwiches, and brinners (breakfasts for dinner). As I got older, my level of confidence grew in the kitchen and I started cooking more meals from scratch. I got inspiration from things I learned from Mom, as well as from the pages of her spiral-bound cookbooks and recipes cut out of newspapers and magazines. And from time to time, I would pick a recipe to cook and surprise her with or I'd find one that we could cook together during the weekend.

As Mom continued to navigate through her career, her job required that she travel more. This ignited her passion for eating out. She was always excited to try new restaurants, telling me how important she thought it was to expose me to different cuisines and cultures. She didn't realize then that she would be the catalyst for jump-starting my appetite, curiosity, and love for exploring and experimenting with new foods and flavors.

When I went off to college, like a lot of students living on campus, the majority of my meals came from the school cafeteria or local restaurants. But in 1991, my journey with food took a slight turn after I attended a lecture by the rapper KRS-One. I don't remember exactly what he said that day, but it made a big impression on me: By the end of that lecture, I had decided to stop eating pork.

The look on Mom's face when I told her was something less than to be desired. She asked: "What do you mean you don't eat pork anymore?" and then asked, "How in the world are we going to make collard greens without ham hocks?" That was a challenging time! But I understood that this was a change that had an impact on both of us. She had valid questions and I explained to her that this was my own (very) small way of reducing my carbon footprint. It took a little while, but Mom slowly began to be more supportive of my lifestyle change.

Eventually, I lost my desire to eat meat. In 2005 I stopped eating beef and shortly after that I stopped eating poultry. By 2007 I had transitioned to a vegetarian lifestyle, which was not too difficult because I *really* love vegetables. However, I had not anticipated missing seafood, and I struggled with that for a while. So, I listened to my body and ultimately decided that I would continue to eat a plant-forward diet, but I would eat seafood whenever the mood hit me. I was mainly vegetarian (and ate eggs and some dairy products) and ate seafood occasionally, which most would consider a pescatarian lifestyle.

As I evolved (and let's be honest, that's a never-ending process), other aspects of my life changed as well. I was single at the time and actively working on creating a better space for wellness and self-care in

my life. I became more mindful of the people I was surrounded by. I made sure to get the proper amount of sleep, and I maintained a good work-life balance. I started exercising on a regular basis. I traveled more and explored various cities on my bucket list. I went back to school to pursue a degree in graphic design (which reignited my love for photography), and basically focused on things that brought me joy. Which ultimately opened me up to being more receptive to other good things that were to come.

In 2011, I reconnected with Alex (my high school sweetheart), who was living in Louisiana. And let me backtrack briefly: When I met Alex in high school, he was unlike anyone I had ever met. He was so confident and charismatic, even at that age. Alex and I were so young then and things got serious for a while, but life took us in other directions and we eventually went our separate ways. So, it was many years later that our paths aligned again and we decided to meet up for a weekend getaway. Well, that trip changed our lives forever. Shortly after, he joined me in Atlanta, and we've been together ever since.

Alex didn't cook a lot, and I'm certain that it's because I may have taken over the kitchen. (Smile.) But, there were often times when Alex would compare certain dishes I made to those of his grandmother. Or he'd say, "Grandma made the best" this or that. Fortunately, years before, I had an opportunity to spend a little time with his grandmother. And even though we weren't actually related, Grandma always made me feel as though we were. That time with her was extremely precious and comforting, because I didn't have the chance to do that with my grandparents . . . they had all passed.

I recall Grandma getting up early each morning to begin cooking meals for the family. Breakfast, lunch, dinner, or supper (as she would often call it). It was so inspiring to watch her maneuver her way around the kitchen with ease. Everything Grandma cooked was from scratch and she never used a recipe. She cooked by look, smell, and taste, adding a little bit of this and a little bit of that as she went along. And when you tasted her food (goodness!), it was as though you could literally taste the love that she had put in there. I definitely believe there's truth to the saying, "the secret ingredient is love." Grandma inspired me to want to put love into my food. And I cherished the times we spent talking and sitting at her kitchen table, cutting

up collard greens or snapping green beans. Those moments with her taught me about giving through food, love, and pride for your family, and for that, I was grateful.

Alex and I moved to the outskirts of Atlanta in 2013. We immediately fell in love with the neighborhood we moved to, which was another close-knit community (Win-win!) with amazing neighbors. In our community, everyone knows everybody, and we all look out for one another and do for one another as though we were family. It is very similar to the neighborhood where I grew up.

My affinity for cooking grew as we began to settle in. I loved cooking, especially for Alex and for our family, close friends, and neighbors. *We ate good* (as we often say) and shared many memorable times together. Contrary to when I was younger, cooking became less of a necessity or chore and more of an act of love. I began sharing photographs of the dishes that I would make on Facebook and Instagram. And I was a little surprised when people started asking for the recipes. It never really occurred to me that anyone would actually want my recipes. So, after much encouragement from friends and family, I started my blog in 2014 in an effort to share some of my recipes with my friends and family. And as a small homage to Grandma, I named my blog *Supper with Michelle*.

Unlike some food bloggers, I worked a full-time job in human resources during the day and devoted time at night and on the weekends to developing and testing recipes and sharing them on my blog and on various social media platforms. Slowly my community began to grow to the point where I started to feel as though I was making a small difference in other people's lives. More than a million people across the world were welcoming my veggie-enthusiastic recipes into their homes, and that made me so happy.

But in 2019, my world came to a halt when Mom passed away unexpectedly. Although friends and family were extremely caring and supportive, this was the first time in my life that I had ever felt completely alone, and I was overwhelmed with grief. I lost my desire to cook and even when I did, nothing I cooked tasted right. The love in it was missing, and this went on for many months.

When COVID hit in early 2020, cooking at home became a necessity for everyone. At one point I was cooking breakfast, lunch, supper, and snacks! Y'all, I hadn't cooked that much in my entire life! And although I was still grieving on top of all of the turmoil and loss going on in the world, I began doing what I had done years back, redirecting my energy to the things that brought me joy. And as I did that, I could finally start tasting the love coming back into my cooking, and the feeling of joy began to fill our kitchen again.

Life can be full of ups and downs, but *Supper with Love* has been a beautiful journey for me, and I'm so happy and proud to be able to share it. This book is *filled* with comforting, flavorful, and vibrant plant-forward and pescetarian meals that are easily adaptable no matter what your lifestyle is. Nowadays, I find myself leaning on recipes that have been favorites of ours and that I have been making for years, like my Kitchen Sink Enchilada Casserole (page 225) or Mom's Tuna & Egg Salad Sammies (page 149). And then there are recipes that I developed during the pandemic, like my DIY Spicy Tofu Bowls (page 166) or Spicy Lemongrass Tofu with Broccoli (page 222). Or there are recipes inspired by some of my favorite childhood classics, like my Alphabet Soup (for the Big Kid in You) (page 74) and Sunday Night Vegetable Pot Pie (page 221), as well as favorites inspired by restaurants, both local and afar, like my comforting Creamy Spinach & Tomato Orzo (page 214) or Smoky Salmon Chowder (page 128).

The purpose of this book is not to try to get you to stop eating meat. I simply believe in finding a dietary lifestyle that works best for *you*. And equally important is finding a way to maintain a good balance of fruits and vegetables in whatever dietary lifestyle you choose. By providing you with many of my favorite ways to celebrate vegetables, I hope you're inspired to spend more time in the produce section of your grocery store, visit your local farmers' markets, and/or join a local CSA program—ultimately working more vegetables into your everyday meals. And I will be here on the sidelines cheering you on and encouraging you to add a little bit of love into each dish as you welcome these recipes into your homes and make them your own. So, pull up a chair, because you're invited for supper!

A NOTE ABOUT *Mom*

Now that you know a little about my journey, I thought it equally important to tell you a little more about the amazing woman who raised me. Out of respect for her (because she was a really private person) and to protect the privacy of her husband, I will simply refer to her as Mom in this book and not use her name. "Mom" is what everyone called her and now that we are better acquainted, I find it only fitting that you know her as Mom as well.

Mom grew up in Evanston, Illinois, and lived with her mother and grandmother until her teens. She and her mom didn't see eye to eye on a lot of things; because of that, they didn't have the best relationship. The older she got, the more the tension grew. Mom decided to leave home with little to nothing when she was sixteen years old, where she found herself living out on the streets of Chicago for a short period of time. In the 1960s, she joined the Civil Rights Movement and eventually migrated down south to Atlanta. She worked for the Southern Christian Leadership Conference (SCLC) and participated in various sit-ins, protests, and marches with Dr. Martin Luther King, Jr. After the tragic assassination of Dr. King in 1968, she shifted gears entirely and began a career in real estate, eventually moving into banking and later mortgage lending.

It was also during that time that Mom befriended my aunt Harriet, who was my father's half sister. Mom and Harriet became roommates and it was Harriet who introduced Mom to my father, who was originally from Cleveland, Ohio. As you can imagine, interracial relationships were still not looked upon highly back then. Mom was white and my father was Black, and they received scrutiny from all sides and angles. But regardless of what anyone thought or the obstacles they would face, they got married in 1971. Their first child was my sister Dawn, who unfortunately passed away shortly after she was born. Devastated, it was a while before they decided to try again to have another child. But luckily, their desire to be parents was strong and I was born a few years later. As time went on their relationship became quite turbulent (and that's putting it lightly), which ultimately led to their divorce in 1974.

It was years later, in 2001, that Mom met and married the true love of her life. She and her husband built a life together in the Atlanta area. However, it was their longing to live in a city with a slightly slower pace that took them to Charlotte, North Carolina, in 2016. In Mom's spare time, she enjoyed reading, catching up on her favorite TV shows and watching boxing (goodness she *loved* boxing), shopping, going to the movies, eating out, and celebrating *every* occasion, big or small.

In 2019, Mom and her husband made the decision to move to Wilmington, North Carolina. She had dreamed of living near the beach for as long as I could remember, and she was finally making the big move. In May of that year, Alex and I drove up to North Carolina to help them pack, move, and get settled into their new place. The night before we left to drive back to Atlanta, Mom and I had a heart-to-heart talk. She told me how proud she was of me, and my heart felt extremely heavy as I felt tears flowing from my eyes. I was happy that she had finally made it to the beach, but I was sad that I was leaving so soon. I told her that I looked forward to walking the beach with her the next time we came up, and I gave her the biggest hug and kiss before Alex and I hit the road to drive back to Atlanta early the next morning. On our way back, Mom called while we were driving. She told me that she and her husband had driven out to the beach that day for a nice meal and I could hear the pure happiness in her voice, which made me feel at peace.

Not long after getting home, a series of unexpected and traumatic events took place and Mom had to be rushed to the hospital. In shock, I immediately drove back up to North Carolina. Rushing through the doors of the hospital, I honestly thought that everything would be okay . . . and that we'd leave the hospital with Mom. Unfortunately, that was not the case. There was nothing that the doctors could do and she passed away just a few days later. As I'm sure many of you can relate, grief is *hard*, and healing takes time. But love—especially the love of someone dear to you—lasts forever.

It's amazing how and what Mom continues to teach me. How I can still hear her saying, "Hi dear, it's your mother" or "Hi Sweetie!" or "I love you," although I can't actually *hear* her voice. It wasn't until I started writing this book that so many things really began

to click. How so many fond memories that I have of her were of times shared over a warm meal eating at one of our favorite restaurants or of our family eating together. Mom was my number one fan. She would always ask how my blog was going—and she encouraged me to write a cookbook. So, this one's for her. I know it would have made her so freaking happy and tremendously proud.

A FEW OF MY *Favorite Things*

I'm sure a lot of you have your own arsenal of tools, cookware, and small appliances that make life easier for you. Maybe you started with hand-me-down pots and pans, like me. Or you received an eleven-piece cookware set as a housewarming gift. Either of these is a great starting point because there is no right or wrong way to build your kitchen.

When selecting things for my kitchen I try to be thoughtful and intentional in my selection process. I select things that, as author and TV host Marie Kondo would say, "spark joy." I love vibrant colors, and finding colorful pots to add to my collection makes me happy. However, there are some basic things that I think are essential in the kitchen: a chef's knife, paring knife, serrated bread knife, heat-resistant silicone spatula, ladle, tongs, wooden spoons, Microplane, vegetable peeler, box grater, fine-mesh sieve, colander, large cutting board, measuring cups, measuring spoons, skillets and saucepans of various sizes, sheet pans, baking dishes, and mixing bowls.

Here are some of my favorite things that I feel deserve an honorable mention:

1. When making salad dressing, condiments, dips, spreads, and sauces, a **high-powered blender** or an 8- or 10-cup **food processor** (for larger jobs) and a **small blender** such as a Nutribullet (for smaller jobs) are key. For those things that can easily be shaken and stored in the same container, I reuse **jelly jars**, and I have **mason** and **Weck jars** with lids.

2. A **citrus handpress** for juicing lemons and limes. Yes, you can certainly squeeze and strain the lemon juice through your hand, but you get far more juice when using this.

3. When preparing salads, I use a **large bowl**, one of those large stainless steel ones. Particularly, one that is larger than the amount of ingredients in my salads, so that I have a lot of room to toss the mixture without ingredients falling out of the bowl.

4. A **Dutch oven, large cast-iron skillet,** and a **braiser** kind of go hand-in-hand, in my opinion. Dutch ovens and braisers can be a little pricey, but if you take care of them, quality pieces will last a lifetime.

5. For soup that requires a little bit of blending such as my Sunshine Dal (page 77), Cream of Asparagus Soup (page 106), and Comforting Broccoli-Cheddar Soup (page 109), I highly recommend an **immersion blender**. It gives you better control over what you're blending, and you don't have to worry about ladling hot liquids into your stand blender.

6. I've always had an affinity for handcrafted **everyday bowls**, particularly the shallow and wide kind. Over the years I've built quite a beautiful collection and I eat almost every meal in one, if it will fit. They are so great to have on hand whether it be for soup, salad, grain bowls, pasta, etc.

7. I love my **tofu press** and definitely recommend having one if you eat tofu often. However, if you don't own a tofu press, here's another way to press out excess water:

> **HOW TO PRESS TOFU:** Wrap the tofu with a clean kitchen towel and place it on a plate or lay several paper towels on a plate, place the tofu down, and then wrap two more paper towels on top and around the tofu. Then put something weighted such as a Dutch oven on top and let that sit on the tofu for 15 to 30 minutes. This will release or press a lot of moisture out of the tofu.

A PEEK INTO MY *Pantry*

I have a confession to make: I love peeking into other people's spice cabinets, pantries, and fridges. Believe it or not, it's quite fascinating to me. It's kind of like if you were to show me all the stamps in your passport, places that you've been, but through the world of spices and ingredients. It's a way for me to understand the kind of food journeys you've been on. Well, this is me opening my spice cabinet and pantry to you.

Acids/Vinegars/Spirits: I always have lemons and limes on hand and various types of vinegar. You will see them used in a lot of different ways in this book. Pickle and olive juices are great as well. Instead of pouring those down the sink, consider using them in salad dressings. I also try to keep a can or two of lager beer on hand because I never know when I may want to make a beer batter to fry up some veggies. Last, a good bottle of red and white wine to cook with. I love to use wine when deglazing for additional flavor, which you'll see done in several recipes in this book. Some wines are processed using animal products so be sure to check the label if you're wanting to avoid using animal products. The list of vegan wine manufacturers is expanding, but one of my favorites is Frey Vineyards. If you don't drink or cook with alcohol, you can substitute vegetable broth or water for the wine.

Cheese: My love for cheese is undying. When selecting cheese, I find it most beneficial to read the label, especially those of you who prefer to eat vegetarian-friendly cheese. Most vegetarian-friendly cheese will state whether microbial enzymes, vegetarian enzymes, or vegetable- or plant-based rennet, as opposed to animal rennet, were used when it was produced. There are so many different brands out now that offer vegetarian-friendly and nondairy cheeses; for example, BelGioioso has a vegetarian parmesan cheese that I enjoy using. In many of the recipes that call for cheese, it can be omitted or nondairy cheeses such as feta, mozzarella, and parmesan can be substituted. Some of the vegan brands I use are Boursin, Daiya, Field Roast Chao, Follow Your Heart, Kite Hill, Miyoko's Creamery, Trader Joe's, Treeline Cheeses, Violife, and 365 Whole Foods.

Condiments: If you open our fridge or cabinets, you'll find capers, chow chow, chutney, Dijon mustard, fire-roasted red bell peppers, ketchup, kimchi, various types of olives, pepperoncini, pickles, preserved lemons, relishes, sauerkraut, sun-dried tomatoes, whole-grain mustard, and yellow mustard. As for mayonnaise, I'm a Hellmann's fan, so anytime mayonnaise is listed as an ingredient, that's the brand I use. Another favorite is Kewpie, which is a Japanese mayonnaise. If you've never had it, Kewpie is creamy in texture and has a slightly eggy-tangy flavor profile.

Fats/Oils: The oils that get the most use in my house are extra-virgin olive oil (a less expensive kind for sautéing and roasting, and a "good" extra-virgin olive oil for salad dressings and finishing dishes), hot chili oil, cooking oil spray, and toasted sesame oil. When it comes to butter, I prefer to use unsalted so I have control over the quantity of salt used. I use ghee and coconut oil sparingly, only for certain dishes where it's preferable for their flavors to shine through. I use neutral oils, primarily canola oil and vegetable oil, as well. If you prefer to use less oil, sauté vegetables in a tablespoon or two of water or vegetable broth instead, and when baking or roasting vegetables, use silicone baking mats or parchment paper so that your vegetables do not stick to your sheet pan.

Fresh Herbs: There's nothing quite like the taste of fresh herbs, and I try to use them whenever possible because they help brighten up almost any dish. If I call for dried herbs, a small handful of fresh herbs can certainly be used instead. If you have leftover herbs from dishes that you make, I encourage you to use them in other things such as butter, chermoula, Chimichurri Sauce (page 196), chutney, dipping sauces, gremolata, Basil Pesto (page 145), pistou (see Michelle's Tip on page 145), salad dressing, salsa verde, and Zhoug (page 231).

Other Dairy Products: Crème fraîche, mascarpone, plain yogurt, and sour cream are all great for salad dressings, soups, and sauces.

Plant-Based Products: Things have come so far as it relates to all of the vegan and plant-based products that are now being sold in stores and offered in restaurants. You can find plant-based bacon, chicken, deli slices, ground beef, meatballs, pepperoni, sausage, etc. You can also find an array of nondairy products, such as cream cheese, egg substitutes (such as JUST Egg), sour cream, and mayonnaise. There's even vegan Worcestershire sauce. I realize that it's a different approach to cooking and that it may not be for everyone, but I wanted to incorporate these products into a few of my recipes, such as my For the Love of Hash Browns Casserole (page 156), Hearty Vegetarian Chili (page 96), and my Vegetarian Zuppa Toscana (page 105). Do I cook with or eat these types of products often? Only when the mood strikes, like anything else. New products are popping up all of the time, but some of the brands I use on occasion are Field Roast, Gardein, Hodo Foods, Impossible Foods, Lightlife, MorningStar Farms, Quorn, Sweet Earth, and Tofurky. If you prefer not to use these products, the headnotes and **Freestyle It** section of the recipes offer other delicious alternatives.

Roots and Bulbs: I use a lot of onions and garlic. Ginger, turmeric, shallots, and scallions get a lot of love as well. If you don't eat onions, fennel and celery are often good substitutes, depending on the dish. If you don't eat garlic, you can certainly omit it if you choose. But also consider things like fresh chives, a little horseradish sauce, ginger, or even lemon zest to help boost flavor when appropriate.

Salt: I've cooked with fine sea salt for years and it is the primary variety I used when developing the recipes for this book. I use Diamond Crystal kosher salt on occasion, along with Maldon when I need a flaky finishing salt. Also note that in many of the recipes I do not include specific measurements for salt—I prefer for you to determine what tastes best to you. When adding salt, I suggest tasting first and then adding a small amount at a time—it's a lot harder to correct something that's been oversalted.

Sauces and Pastes: I love sauces, pastes, dips, and spreads because they help to bring the flava! These are the ones I use most in this book: anchovy paste, Calabrian chili peppers, curry paste, fish sauce, harissa paste, hot sauce (Texas Pete and Frank's RedHot), liquid smoke, miso, salsa, Sriracha sauce, tahini (Soom), tamari (San-J), Thai sweet chili sauce, and Worcestershire sauce. A few others I enjoy are BBQ sauce, chili crisp (Fly by Jing), gochujang, hoisin sauce, ponzu, sambal oelek, and tomatillo sauce. A tube of tomato paste is also essential. I prefer using tubes because you can squeeze out the exact amount of tomato paste that you need. But if you use cans, spoon out tablespoon portions of any leftovers in the can and place them on a sheet pan lined with parchment paper and transfer to the freezer. Once frozen, transfer the portions to a freezer-safe container and store in the freezer to be used in future dishes.

Spices and Seasonings: I have a *large* selection of spices—too many to list here. But I love all of the different worlds that spices can open up. When it comes to spices, I find it important to keep track of the expiration dates; once ground spices are opened, they start to lose their smell and flavor after six months to one year (whole spices last a little longer).

Sweeteners: I use sweeteners such as brown sugar, honey, pure cane sugar, and pure grade A maple syrup in a variety of ways in this book. They balance flavor, whether it is in a salad dressing, sauce, or drizzled here or there.

Other Things in My Kitchen: My pantry also has all-purpose flour, arrowroot or cornstarch, baking powder, baking soda, bamboo shoots, beans and legumes, canned tomatoes, canned vegetables (you'll find frozen vegetables in the freezer, too), chipotle peppers in adobo sauce, coconut milk, cornmeal, dried mushrooms, canned green chilies, grits, kombu, low-sodium vegetable broth (for when I don't have homemade broth on hand), marinara sauce, nori, various types of pastas and noodles, polenta, rice/grains, rolled oats, tinned or jarred fish, and water chestnuts.

AS YOU COOK *(and Dance)* YOUR WAY THROUGH THIS BOOK

Over the years I've had the opportunity to talk to many of you and one of the questions that I always like to ask is, "What are some of the things that you find helpful when reading cookbooks?" I typically get an array of answers, but the ones that stood out the most are things like serving sizes, make ahead suggestions, and ideas or variations for ingredients to swap in or out in recipes. So, with this book I tried to incorporate some of those things (along with a few others) to help guide you and set the vibe as you cook (and dance) your way through this book.

A Soundtrack to the Recipe

 Listening to music while I cook plays a major role in setting the tone and mood for how I maneuver through the kitchen. It's like a soundtrack to the recipe or meal that I'm preparing. So, if you don't already do this, try putting on your favorite song, artist, or playlist. Dance (if you can) and sing with your favorite wooden spoon in hand, slide across the kitchen (dance) floor, and have fun with it! I took a little time to develop a playlist of music that I love and it will give you the vibe for this book. Using the camera on your cellphone, point it directly at this QR code, tap on the link, and it will take you directly to the *Supper with Love* Spotify playlist, if you'd like to have a listen.

Serving Sizes

The serving sizes in the book are based loosely on how many servings Alex and I typically get from these recipes. Most of the salads serve 2 to 4 people, depending on if you're having the salad as a meal or serving it as a side. The same thing applies to soups, which typically serve 2 to 6 people, depending on if it's a starter or your main. I don't cook a lot of really big meals, but I do have a few dishes that serve a larger crowd sprinkled in and those feed up to 8 people.

Make Ahead This is my little way of suggesting to make certain things ahead of time or to do various steps first so that it doesn't seem like so much when you actually start preparing the recipe—things like boiling eggs and making salad dressings, quick pickles, sauces, condiments, etc.

Michelle's Tip Some of my methods may not be "traditional." My methods are a distillation of knowledge I've picked up along the way—from watching Mom cook and from friends and family who I've cooked with in their kitchens. I use this section to share additional information. It could be a helpful kitchen tip, ways to repurpose leftovers, etc.

Freestyle it The wonderful thing about this book is that a lot of the recipes are versatile, which means you can easily add your own flair to them. You will see a **Freestyle It** section with some of the recipes. This is where I provide suggestions for alternate ingredients that can be used. It's my way of encouraging you to get into your groove by changing up ingredients based on your personal preferences, dietary lifestyle, what you have on hand, or the produce that is in season. Have I tried all the things I suggest? No. But they are ingredients that I think are good alternatives. Just keep in mind that cook times and temperatures may vary when substituting ingredients. And when it comes to soup, the amount of broth needed may differ from the recipe, depending on the ingredient that you're substituting.

Veganize it Whether you want to cut down on your meat consumption, you're vegan or flexitarian, or you just prefer to be dairy- and fish-free, I think it's helpful to know simple ways to make meals vegan (if they are not already vegan), thus this section. It could be as simple as omitting cheese in a recipe or by using work-arounds such as vegan mayonnaise, vegan cheese, nondairy milk, nondairy yogurt, or tofu.

Salads

A LOVE LANGUAGE

Leafy green salads, pasta salads, grain salads, bean salads, fruity salads, warm salads! I love them all! For this chapter, I wanted to equip you with a variety of homemade salad dressings and vinaigrettes that I typically pair these salads with. When making most of these salad dressings, I usually start with a small amount of salt, especially when there may be other savory ingredients in the salad such as proteins, olives, or cheese. I recommend doing a taste test by pouring a little bit of the salad dressing or vinaigrette on the leafy green, pasta, or grain that you're using. Ask yourself if it needs more herbs, oil, mayonnaise, yogurt, vinegar, citrus, mustard, salt, miso, tamari, anchovies, honey, maple syrup . . . you get the picture. Keep in mind as you're tasting that some salad dressings may be sweeter than others and may need a little salt to offset some of the sweetness, or vice versa. The key is finding a good balance that tastes good to you. Also, I use various types of vinegars/acids that are interchangeable in a lot of cases. If you want to swap out red wine vinegar for lemon juice, feel free to do so. The only one I don't recommend replacing in recipes is balsamic vinegar.

CAESAR SALAD—STUFFED

Potatoes

Serves 2

Caesar Dressing (recipe follows)

2 medium to large russet potatoes, cleaned well

Extra-virgin olive oil

Kosher salt to taste

3 cups (195 g) packed stemmed thinly sliced curly or lacinato kale

3 cups (165 g) packed thinly sliced romaine lettuce

2 tablespoons freshly shaved parmesan cheese, plus more for finishing

Unsalted butter (optional)

Freshly ground black pepper to taste (optional)

Growing up, we would often have "baked potato and salad nights" where we would throw a couple of potatoes into the oven and make a nice salad while they were baking. I always found myself pushing the salad toward the potato to kind of get it all into one forkful. Well with this baby, the salad and the baked potato are combined! For the baked potatoes, I like to rub a little olive oil on them and sprinkle them with salt. Which is absolutely perfect if you're the kind of person who enjoys eating the potato skins, like me. To add a little texture to the salad, I use both kale and romaine here, but you can easily use one or the other. If you're not an anchovy fan or want to make the dressing vegan or vegetarian, simply substitute 2 tablespoons capers for the anchovies.

Make Ahead Make the dressing as directed and refrigerate until serving.

Preheat the oven to 425°F (220°C). Line a large sheet pan with parchment paper.

Cook the potatoes: Place the potatoes on the lined pan. Puncture the ends of each potato with a fork and drizzle the potatoes with a little olive oil. Massage the oil in and season each potato generously with salt. Transfer the sheet pan to the oven and bake until soft (put on your oven glove and give the potatoes a squeeze to determine this), 1 hour to 1 hour 15 minutes. When the potatoes are cooked, carefully brush a little bit of the salt off and transfer to a serving plate. Set aside until cool enough to handle.

About 15 minutes before the potatoes are done cooking, combine the kale, romaine lettuce, and parmesan in a large bowl. Pour in just enough dressing to thoroughly coat the leaves. (There will be some left over.) Use a pair of tongs to gently toss the salad to coat. Cover and refrigerate until the potatoes are cooked.

Once the potatoes are cool enough to handle, make a lengthwise slit in each potato. Holding each side, squeeze inward and upward to push the inside up just a bit. Use a fork to fluff the inside of the potato and add butter (if using).

Assemble the potatoes: Use a pair of tongs to serve a generous overflowing portion of the salad over the potatoes along with some freshly shaved parmesan and a few grinds of black pepper if desired. (Look at your masterpiece!) Place the remaining dressing on the table, just in case either of you wants more.

Freestyle it

Other ideas to consider: This salad is also great served over warm flatbread as well as by itself with Herby Croutons (page 133) or crispy chickpeas.

Veganize it

Use nondairy butter and veganize the Caesar Dressing (recipe follows).

RECIPE CONTINUES →

CAESAR DRESSING

Makes about 1¼ cups (300 ml)

1 cup (225 g) mayonnaise

1½ ounces (42 g) freshly grated parmesan cheese (about ½ cup)

3 tablespoons fresh lemon juice (about 1½ medium lemons)

5 oil-packed anchovies or 2½ tablespoons anchovy paste

1 garlic clove, minced

1½ teaspoons Worcestershire sauce

1 teaspoon Dijon mustard

¼ teaspoon ground black pepper, plus more to taste

A few dashes of hot sauce, such as Texas Pete (optional)

Fine sea salt to taste

Combine the mayonnaise, grated parmesan, lemon juice, anchovies, garlic, Worcestershire sauce, mustard, black pepper, hot sauce, and salt in a small food processor or high-powered blender. Blend on high speed or process until smooth and creamy, about 30 seconds. If the dressing is too thick, add water 1 tablespoon at a time to thin it out. Give it a taste and add more salt and pepper, if needed. Pour the dressing into an airtight container and store in the refrigerator until ready to serve. This dressing will keep in the refrigerator for up to 4 days. It may thicken with time; thin it with a little cool water, as needed.

Veganize it

Use vegan mayonnaise, vegan parmesan cheese, and vegan Worcestershire sauce. Omit the anchovies and use 2 tablespoons of capers in their place.

SALAD
with Creamy Herb Dressing

Serves 2 to 4

I've always dreamed of owning two properties: one on or really near the beach . . . and then the other on several acres of land that look out on a beautiful pasture. I'd have a nice size field where I could grow my own food. I'd have a greenhouse and all kinds of fruit trees. And maybe a few smaller farm animals. Until then, I rely on all of the hard-working farmers and farmworkers out there who make farm-to-table meals possible . . . and this salad is a result of that. I'm a big fan of adding raw corn and yellow squash to salads. When in season, they are both so sweet and add a nice little crunch to each bite. And I'm sure you will think of other vegetables that will be perfect to add in as well. As for the eggs, you can certainly dice them if that's easier, but I prefer grating them on top in a small haystack. They become so light and fluffy and sort of melt in with the other ingredients. The star of the salad is the dressing. It's creamy, herbaceous, and slightly tangy, and it pulls all of these ingredients together, resulting in a wonderful combination.

Make Ahead
Hard-boil the eggs as directed in the recipe. Refrigerate until the salad is ready to be assembled. Make the creamy herb dressing as directed and refrigerate until serving.

In a large serving bowl, combine the mesclun, corn, tomatoes, cucumber, carrot, squash, and sunflower seeds. Use a pair of tongs to toss several times. Crack and peel each egg (see Michelle's Tip). Carefully grate the boiled eggs on top of the salad using the medium holes of a box grater. (Remember that haystack I referred to.) Throw in those small pieces that are too small to grate as well. Season lightly with salt and pepper, if desired, and give the salad a toss. Serve immediately in individual bowls and allow everyone to drizzle several tablespoons of creamy herb dressing (there may be some left over) on top of their salads.

Veganize it
Omit the eggs and veganize the Creamy Herb Dressing (recipe follows).

RECIPE CONTINUES →

2 or 3 large Hard-Boiled Eggs (recipe follows; use 3 if feeding more than 2 people)

Creamy Herb Dressing (recipe follows)

5 ounces (140 g) mesclun or your favorite leafy greens

Kernels from 1 ear fresh yellow corn (½ cup/72 g cooked corn, if making off-season)

¾ cup (135 g) diced tomatoes

½ medium English cucumber, roughly chopped (about 1 cup/65 g)

1 small carrot, peeled and coarsely shredded (about ⅓ cup/35 g)

1 small young yellow squash, cut into matchsticks (about ½ cup/50 g)

2 tablespoons raw or roasted sunflower seeds

Fine sea salt and freshly ground black pepper to taste (optional)

Michelle's Tip

My method for peeling eggs: Once the boiled eggs have cooled and the water is drained from the saucepan, clang the eggs back and forth inside the saucepan until all sides of the eggs are cracked. You should then be able to easily peel and remove the shells from the eggs. Run the peeled eggs under cold water to get rid of any small pieces of shell remaining.

HARD-BOILED EGGS

Makes as many as you want

Large eggs

Fill a medium saucepan with water, enough to cover the eggs by several inches, and bring to a boil over medium heat. Once the water is boiling, carefully lower the eggs into the water with a slotted spoon. Boil for 12 minutes. Drain off the hot water and carefully run the pan under cold water until the eggs are cool to the touch. Serve or refrigerate for up to 1 week.

CREAMY HERB DRESSING

Makes about 1¼ cups (300 ml)

½ cup (15 g) loosely packed cilantro leaves and tender stems
⅓ cup (15 g) roughly chopped fresh chives
½ cup (115 g) plain yogurt or sour cream
½ cup (112 g) mayonnaise
2 tablespoons distilled white vinegar
¼ teaspoon ground black pepper, plus more to taste
1 small garlic clove, peeled but whole
Fine sea salt to taste
1 tablespoon minced fresh dill

Combine the cilantro, chives, yogurt, mayonnaise, vinegar, black pepper, garlic, and salt in a small food processor or high-powered blender. Blend on high speed or process until smooth, about 30 seconds. If the dressing is too thick, add water 1 tablespoon at a time to thin to the desired consistency. Stir in the fresh dill. Give it a taste and add more salt and pepper, if needed. Pour the dressing into a small airtight container and store in the refrigerator until ready to serve. This dressing will keep in the refrigerator for up to 4 days.

Freestyle it

Substitutions for cilantro: basil, flat-leaf parsley

Veganize it

Use nondairy plain yogurt or vegan sour cream and vegan mayonnaise.

Strawberry & Halloumi SALAD

with Creamy Balsamic Dressing

Serves 2 to 4

Creamy Balsamic Dressing (recipe follows)

1 tablespoon canola oil

8 ounces (225 g) Halloumi cheese, patted dry with a paper towel and cut into slices ¼ inch (6 mm) thick

5 ounces (140 g) mesclun or mixed field greens

1 medium avocado, sliced

8 ounces (225 g) strawberries, sliced

⅓ cup (35 g) pecan halves

Originating from the island of Cyprus, Halloumi is by far one of my favorite types of cheese. I realize it may be hard to find for some of you, and I've provided some other options, but if you can get your hands on it, give it a try. It's a little bit salty and offsets the natural sweetness in this salad so well. And although strawberries are available in most markets throughout the year, I highly recommend making this salad when strawberries are in peak season. Feel free to swap out the fruit based on what's in season.

Make Ahead Make the creamy balsamic dressing as directed and refrigerate until serving.

Cook the Halloumi: Heat the canola oil in a large nonstick skillet over medium heat. Put the Halloumi in the skillet and fry until both sides are golden in color, 3 to 5 minutes, flipping once. Transfer the Halloumi to a plate to cool slightly. Once the Halloumi has cooled, break it into bite-size pieces (and if you're like me, snack on a piece or two while you prepare the salad).

Assemble the salad: Add the mesclun to a large serving platter or in a bowl and top with the Halloumi, avocado, strawberries, and pecans. Drizzle the creamy balsamic dressing lightly over the top to coat the leaves (there will be some left over) and serve immediately.

Freestyle it

Substitutions for Halloumi: feta, goat cheese, paneer, or parmesan

Substitutions for mesclun: arugula, baby kale, frisée, spinach, or watercress

Substitutions for strawberries: apricots, blackberries, blueberries, cherries, figs, nectarines, peaches, persimmons, or raspberries

Substitutions for pecans: almonds, hazelnuts, pistachios, or walnuts

Veganize it

Use vegan feta cheese and veganize the Creamy Balsamic Dressing (recipe follows) by using vegan mayonnaise.

CREAMY BALSAMIC DRESSING

Makes about ¾ cup (175 ml)

¼ cup (55 g) plus 2 tablespoons mayonnaise

¼ cup (60 ml) balsamic vinegar

1 tablespoon pure maple syrup

½ teaspoon Italian seasoning

¼ teaspoon garlic powder

¼ teaspoon fine sea salt, plus more as needed

⅛ teaspoon ground black pepper, plus more as needed

Combine 1 tablespoon water, the mayonnaise, balsamic, maple syrup, oregano, garlic powder, salt, and black pepper in a blender or small food processor. Blend on high speed or process until smooth and creamy, about 30 seconds. Give it a taste and add more salt and pepper, if needed. Pour the dressing into a small airtight container and store in the refrigerator until ready to serve. This dressing will keep in the refrigerator for up to 4 days. It may thicken with time; thin it with a little cool water, as needed.

Marinated White Bean
& HEIRLOOM TOMATO SALAD

Serves 4

In 2018, I ran my first half-marathon in Savannah, Georgia. It was quite a major feat for me because for years I had told myself I can't run. But after some encouragement from Alex (or him telling me to remove the word "can't" from my vocabulary), I began to run. It took a while to build up my endurance—first a half mile, then a mile—until I had slowly worked my way up to six miles. I trained a lot and joined the Black Girls RUN! group on Facebook for some added motivation. Then in 2014, I ran my very first 10K race, the Atlanta Journal-Constitution Peachtree Road Race. And I've been running that race along with a few others ever since. Typically, on long-run days I come home and refuel with simple salads like this. One thing I love about this salad is that it comes together rather quickly, aside from the time it takes for the beans to marinate. This can be prepared anytime of the year, but I particularly enjoy making it when heirloom tomatoes are at their peak. If heirloom tomatoes are not available or in season, use a different variety of ripe tomatoes.

Make Ahead

Make the vinaigrette: Combine the vinegar, basil, oregano, mustard, and garlic in a large bowl. Season with salt and pepper and whisk in the olive oil until thoroughly incorporated. Set aside until ready to use. This vinaigrette will keep in the refrigerator for up to 1 week when stored in an airtight container.

Assemble the salad: Add the cannellini beans and red onion to the bowl with the vinaigrette. Gently toss the vinaigrette with the bean mixture. Cover and let the mixture marinate at room temperature for at least 30 minutes.

Add the mozzarella, tomatoes, and arugula and give the salad a light toss. Taste, add salt as needed, and serve immediately.

Veganize it

Omit the mozzarella cheese balls or use vegan mozzarella cheese.

WHITE BALSAMIC VINAIGRETTE

3 tablespoons white balsamic vinegar

½ teaspoon dried basil

½ teaspoon dried oregano

½ teaspoon stone-ground Dijon mustard

1 small garlic clove, finely grated

Fine sea salt and freshly ground black pepper to taste

3 tablespoons extra-virgin olive oil

SALAD

1 (15-ounce/425 g) can cannellini beans, drained and rinsed, or 1½ cups/277 g home-cooked beans

¼ cup (30g) thinly sliced red onion

8 ounces (225 g) ciliegine mozzarella cheese balls (cherry size), drained and halved

2 cups (260 g) diced heirloom tomatoes or vine-ripened tomatoes

2 cups (40 g) loosely packed baby arugula

Fine sea salt to taste

Freestyle it

Substitutions for cannellini beans: brown lentils, chickpeas, corona beans, Great Northern beans, navy beans

Substitutions for baby arugula: baby kale, frisée, spinach, watercress

Other ideas to consider: Use 2 cups of croutons or 1 cup of farro or wheat berries instead of mozzarella; roasted squash or sweet potatoes instead of tomatoes.

PORTOBELLO MUSHROOM SALAD

with Shallot Vinaigrette

Serves 2 to 4

Shallot Vinaigrette (recipe follows)

MUSHROOMS

2 tablespoons canola oil

12 ounces (340 g) cremini mushrooms, halved if small, quartered if large

1 tablespoon (15 g) unsalted butter

1 teaspoon Montreal steak seasoning (such as McCormick), plus more to taste

1 teaspoon Worcestershire sauce

Fine sea salt and freshly ground black pepper to taste

SALAD

4 small heads Little Gem lettuce, roughly chopped (about 6 cups)

½ pint cherry tomatoes, halved (about 1 cup/150 g)

½ medium English cucumber, thinly sliced (about 1 cup/65 g)

1½ ounces (42 g) blue cheese, crumbled (about ⅓ cup)

This is my take on the classic black and blue steak salad that I enjoyed back in my steak-eating days, but I use mushrooms as a substitute. Mushrooms have this "meaty" texture going on and once they absorb whatever marinade or sauce you cook them in, it really helps to bring out their umami flavors. They become so flavorful and juicy and are perfect on top of this familiar classic. Every time Alex eats this salad, he always says "Mmm!" Which as you know is one of the biggest compliments. Mushrooms are one of his faves and he loves it when I prepare them this way.

Make Ahead Make the shallot vinaigrette as directed at least 30 minutes ahead and refrigerate until serving.

Cook the mushrooms: Heat the canola oil in a large cast-iron or nonstick skillet over medium-high heat. Once shimmering, place the mushrooms in the skillet, evenly distributed, with most of the cut sides down. Cook undisturbed until they are a deep golden color, about 5 minutes. Add the butter, steak seasoning, and Worcestershire sauce and give the mushrooms a stir. Cook until browned all over, 3 to 4 minutes. Taste and add salt, black pepper, and additional steak seasoning, if needed. Remove the skillet from the heat and let the mushrooms cool slightly.

Assemble the salad: Arrange the lettuce on a large platter or on individual serving plates. Add the tomatoes, cucumber, blue cheese, and mushrooms. Drizzle on just enough shallot vinaigrette to evenly coat the salad (there may be some left over) and serve immediately with the remaining vinaigrette on the side for anyone who would like more.

Freestyle it

Substitutions for Little Gem lettuce: arugula, baby kale, frisée, mesclun, romaine, spinach

Substitutions for blue cheese: feta, goat cheese, Gorgonzola, parmesan, ricotta salata

Veganize it

Use nondairy butter, vegan Worcestershire sauce or tamari, and vegan feta or blue cheese. Veganize the Shallot Vinaigrette (recipe follows).

SHALLOT VINAIGRETTE

Makes about ¾ cup (175 ml)

1 small shallot, finely diced

½ cup (120 ml) extra-virgin olive oil

½ cup (120 ml) red wine vinegar

1 tablespoon honey

½ teaspoon Italian seasoning

½ teaspoon garlic powder

¼ teaspoon ground black pepper

Fine sea salt to taste

Combine the shallot, olive oil, vinegar, honey, Italian seasoning, garlic powder, black pepper, and salt in a small screw-top jar. Put on the lid and shake vigorously until thoroughly incorporated. Give it a taste and season with more salt, if needed. Let the shallots marinate in the dressing for 30 to 45 minutes prior to serving. This vinaigrette will keep in the refrigerator for up to 5 days. (The oil will solidify once refrigerated. Let it sit at room temperature for 15 to 30 minutes to allow the oil to liquefy before using.)

Veganize it

Use pure maple syrup instead of honey.

Parmesan, Arugula & Pear
SALAD
with Maple-Dijon Vinaigrette

Serves 2 to 4

Maple Dijon Vinaigrette (recipe follows)

6 cups (120 g) loosely packed baby arugula

1 small d'Anjou or Bartlett pear, cored and thinly sliced

⅓ cup (32 g) sliced almonds, raw or toasted (see Michelle's Tip)

1 ounce (28 g) freshly shaved parmesan cheese (about ⅓ cup)

Fine sea salt and freshly ground black pepper to taste

1 medium avocado, thinly sliced

Known for being a little "peppery," arugula is what really makes this salad work. It offers the perfect balance along with the subtle sweetness from the pear, the saltiness from the shaved parmesan cheese, the creaminess from the avocado, and the crunch from the almonds. To switch things up a bit, I occasionally like to toss on a crispy fried egg or two, which may sound a bit odd . . . but it's really yummy.

Make Ahead

Make the maple Dijon vinaigrette as directed and refrigerate until serving.

Combine the arugula, pear, almonds, and parmesan in a large bowl. Drizzle on just enough of the vinaigrette to evenly coat the salad (there will be some left over) and give it a light toss. Taste and season with salt and pepper, if needed. Arrange on a beautiful large serving platter or in individual serving bowls with the avocado slices on top and serve immediately with the remaining dressing on the side.

Veganize it
Omit the parmesan or use vegan parmesan cheese.

Freestyle it

Substitutions for arugula: baby kale, frisée, radicchio, spinach, tender dandelion greens, watercress

Substitutions for pears: apples, blackberries, blueberries, cantaloupe, cherries, figs, grapes, nectarines, oranges, peaches, persimmons, raspberries, strawberries, watermelon

Substitutions for almonds: hazelnuts, macadamia nuts, pecans, pine nuts, pistachios, walnuts

Substitutions for parmesan: Asiago, Gruyère, Manchego, Pecorino Romano

MAPLE DIJON VINAIGRETTE

Makes about ¾ cup (180 ml)

½ cup (120 ml) extra-virgin olive oil

¼ cup (60 ml) apple cider vinegar or champagne vinegar

2 teaspoons stone-ground Dijon mustard

2 teaspoons pure maple syrup

½ teaspoon Italian seasoning

½ teaspoon garlic powder

¼ teaspoon ground black pepper, plus more to taste

Pinch of red chile flakes (optional)

Fine sea salt to taste

Michelle's Tip

To toast almonds, set a large skillet over medium heat. Spread the nuts in the skillet in a single layer and toast until slightly golden in color, 3 to 5 minutes.

Combine the olive oil, vinegar, mustard, maple syrup, Italian seasoning, garlic powder, black pepper, chile flakes (if using), and salt in a small screw-top jar. Put on the lid and shake vigorously until thoroughly incorporated. Give it a taste and season with more salt and pepper, if needed. Set aside or refrigerate until ready to use. This vinaigrette will keep in the refrigerator for up to 1 week. (The oil will solidify once refrigerated. Let it sit at room temperature for 15 to 30 minutes to allow the oil to liquefy before using.)

CHICKPEA-ORZO SALAD

Serves 4 to 6

Your Dekalb Farmers Market is one of the largest farmers' markets in the Atlanta area and I love shopping there. They have *everything*! One section of the market that I always hit up is the deli, because they have such a wonderful selection of fresh salads, sauces, and pickles. One salad that I particularly love is their curried chickpea-orzo salad, and yes, I had to create a variation of it. This salad is sweet, tangy, savory, and so flavorful!

Make the vinaigrette: Combine the olive oil, vinegar, maple syrup, curry powder, garlic powder, and salt in a large glass or metal mixing bowl (one that won't stain from the curry powder). Whisk vigorously and set aside.

Prepare the pasta and chickpeas: Bring a medium saucepan of salted water to a boil over medium-high heat. Stir in the pasta and cook according to the package directions.

Meanwhile, combine the broth and chickpeas in a small saucepan. Cook over medium heat for about 8 minutes to slightly infuse the flavor of the chickpeas with the vegetable broth; time this so that they are finished when the pasta is ready.

Once the pasta is tender, drain and transfer to the large bowl of dressing. Drain the chickpeas and add to the bowl with the orzo. Stir to thoroughly combine with the orzo and vinaigrette and let cool.

Make the salad: Add the raisins, bell pepper, shallot, and cilantro to the orzo-chickpea mixture. Mix well, taste, and add more salt as needed. Cover and refrigerate for 30 minutes to allow the flavors to marry. Serve and enjoy!

CURRY VINAIGRETTE

¼ cup (60 ml) extra-virgin olive oil

¼ cup (60 ml) apple cider vinegar

1 tablespoon pure maple syrup

1½ teaspoons mild yellow curry powder

1 teaspoon garlic powder

Fine sea salt to taste

SALAD

Fine sea salt to taste

1 cup (168 g) orzo pasta

2 cups (480 ml) vegetable broth, store-bought or homemade (page 68)

1 (15-ounce/425 g) can chickpeas, drained and rinsed

½ cup (70 g) golden raisins

½ medium red bell pepper, finely diced

1 small shallot, finely diced (about ⅓ cup/47 g)

⅓ cup (10 g) loosely packed fresh cilantro leaves, roughly chopped

Freestyle it

Substitution for shallot: ½ medium red onion

Substitution for cilantro: flat-leaf parsley

CRUNCHY *Kale Salad*
with Lemony Tahini Dressing

Serves 4

Lemony Tahini Dressing (recipe follows)

1 bunch curly kale, stemmed and roughly chopped (about 8 cups/520 g)

1 cup (85 g) broccoli slaw (see Michelle's Tip)

¾ cup (71 g) thinly sliced red cabbage

⅓ cup (32 g) sliced almonds, raw or toasted (see Michelle's Tip, page 38)

½ cup (70 g) dried cranberries

1½ ounces (42 g) blue cheese, preferably smoked, crumbled (about ⅓ cup)

Fine sea salt and freshly ground black pepper to taste

½ cup (28 g) crunchy chow mein noodles, such as La Choy

Freestyle it

Substitutions for almonds: cashews, pecans, pistachios, walnuts

Substitutions for dried cranberries: dates, dried blueberries, dried cherries, golden raisins, pomegranate arils

Substitutions for blue cheese: feta, goat cheese, Gorgonzola, parmesan, ricotta salata

Michelle's Tip

For any leftover broccoli slaw in the package, I recommend adding it to a vegetable stir-fry with noodles or vegetable fried rice. You could also make a coleslaw and throw in some of the leftover red cabbage as well. Or you could make vegetable fritters or pakoras.

I've been making a version of this salad ever since I tried the Fairy Kale Salad at Rawesome Juicery at the Sweet Auburn Curb Market in Atlanta. I've made a few additions because I love a good crunch, and this salad is filled with lots of crunchy bits. As for the dressing, it's one that has been a favorite for years. It's great on so many things, such as roasted or grilled vegetables, wraps, all kinds of bowls, and many types of salads.

Make Ahead

Make the lemon tahini dressing as directed and refrigerate until serving.

Combine the kale, broccoli slaw, cabbage, almonds, cranberries, blue cheese, and salt and pepper in a large serving bowl. Drizzle on just enough dressing (there may be some left over) to evenly coat the salad ingredients and toss several times. Give it a taste and add more dressing, salt, and pepper, if needed. Serve immediately sprinkled with the chow mein noodles.

Veganize it

Omit the blue cheese or use vegan blue cheese or feta cheese.

LEMONY TAHINI DRESSING

Makes about ⅔ cup (160 ml)

¼ cup (60 ml) well-stirred tahini

3 tablespoons fresh lemon juice (about 1½ medium lemons), plus more to taste

2 tablespoons pure maple syrup, plus more to taste

¼ teaspoon garlic powder

¼ teaspoon fine sea salt, plus more to taste

Pinch of cayenne pepper (optional)

Combine 3 tablespoons water and the tahini in a small bowl and whisk vigorously. Once it has thickened, add the lemon juice, maple syrup, garlic powder, salt, and cayenne (if using) and whisk thoroughly. Give it a taste and add more lemon juice, maple syrup, or salt, if needed. If the dressing is too thick, add water 1 tablespoon at a time to thin to desired consistency. Pour the dressing into a small airtight container and store in the refrigerator until ready to use. This dressing will keep in the refrigerator for up to 5 days.

Spring Asparagus
PASTA SALAD
with Sun-Dried Tomato Vinaigrette

Serves 4

Sun-Dried Tomato Vinaigrette (recipe follows)

Fine sea salt to taste

8 ounces (225 g) fusilli or rotini pasta

1 tablespoon extra-virgin olive oil

1 pound (450 g) asparagus, tough ends trimmed, sliced into 1-inch (2.5 cm) pieces

1 (15-ounce/425 g) can chickpeas, drained and rinsed

1 (6-ounce/170 g) jar marinated artichoke hearts, drained and roughly chopped

½ cup (78 g) pitted kalamata olives

2 ounces (55 g) feta cheese, crumbled (about ½ cup)

⅓ cup (42 g) finely diced red onion

A small handful of basil leaves (optional), freshly torn

1 garlic clove, finely grated

Fine sea salt and freshly ground black pepper to taste

As soon as the temperatures start to warm and all the flowers start to bloom, I know it's time to make this salad. Although asparagus is widely available throughout the year in some markets, the true asparagus season is really short at local farmers' markets, so I grab them up as soon as I get the chance. When selecting asparagus, try to find tall slender yet firm stalks with tips that look fresh and still beautifully intact. The wonderful thing about this salad is that it's easily adaptable: You can swap the asparagus out for other vegetables as the seasons change.

Make Ahead
Make the sun-dried tomato vinaigrette as directed and refrigerate until serving.

Cook the pasta and asparagus: Bring a medium saucepan of salted water to a rolling boil over high heat. Stir in the pasta and cook until tender according to the package directions. Drain and transfer to a large bowl to cool.

Heat the olive oil in a large skillet over medium-low heat. Once warmed, add the asparagus and sauté until tender, 5 to 7 minutes. Season lightly with salt and transfer the asparagus to the bowl with the pasta.

Make the pasta salad: Once the pasta and asparagus have cooled, add the chickpeas, artichoke hearts, olives, feta, red onion, basil (if using), and garlic to the large bowl. Drizzle enough of the vinaigrette over the salad to evenly coat the ingredients and toss lightly (you may not need all of it). Give it a taste and add more vinaigrette, salt, and pepper, if needed. Cover and refrigerate for 30 minutes so the flavors can marry. Serve chilled.

Freestyle it

Substitutions for asparagus:
blanched fresh peas; roasted baby broccoli, broccoli, cauliflower, or winter squash; sautéed broccoli rabe, fiddleheads, or haricots verts

Substitutions for chickpeas:
cannellini beans, Great Northern beans, navy beans

Veganize it

Omit the feta cheese or use vegan feta cheese and veganize the Sun-Dried Tomato Vinaigrette (recipe follows).

SUN-DRIED TOMATO VINAIGRETTE

Makes about ¾ cup (180 ml)

3 tablespoons minced drained oil-
    packed sun-dried tomatoes

1 tablespoon honey

½ cup (120 ml) extra-virgin olive oil

¼ cup (60 ml) red wine vinegar

½ teaspoon Italian seasoning

½ teaspoon garlic powder

¼ teaspoon ground black pepper

Fine sea salt to taste

Combine the sun-dried tomatoes, honey, olive oil, vinegar, Italian seasoning, garlic powder, black pepper, and salt in a small jar with a lid. (I prefer this vinaigrette to be on the chunky side, however you can blend it if you'd like a smoother consistency.) Put on the lid and shake vigorously until thoroughly incorporated. (Come on now! Put your hip into it!) Give it a taste and add more salt, if needed. Store in the refrigerator until ready to use. This vinaigrette will keep in the refrigerator for up to 5 days. (The oil will solidify once refrigerated. Let it sit at room temperature for 15 to 30 minutes to allow the oil to liquefy before using.)

Veganize it

Use pure maple syrup instead of honey.

KALE, QUINOA &
Chickpea Salad

Serves 4 to 6

4 cups (260 g) packed stemmed and thinly sliced curly kale

2 tablespoons extra-virgin olive oil, plus more to taste

1 (15-ounce/425 g) can chickpeas, drained and rinsed

1 cup (170 g) cooked quinoa (page 179)

½ medium English cucumber, thinly sliced (about 1 cup/130 g)

½ medium red bell pepper, finely diced

½ cup (75 g) cherry tomatoes or Sungold tomatoes, halved

½ cup (15 g) loosely packed flat-leaf parsley leaves, roughly chopped

⅓ cup (42 g) finely diced red onion

¼ cup (10 g) loosely packed fresh mint leaves, roughly chopped

1½ tablespoons red wine vinegar, plus more to taste

1 small garlic clove, finely grated

Fine sea salt and freshly ground black pepper to taste

Anytime my mother-in-love, Sharon (Alex's mom), comes to visit us or we're in Kentucky visiting the family, she always requests that I make her a kale salad. Now, I know kale sometimes has a reputation for being a little tough, but most people don't give it the attention it deserves. Drizzling the kale with a little olive oil first and massaging it in with your hands really helps to soften the leaves. This salad is inspired by another favorite of mine, tabbouleh. You can totally eat this by its lonesome, but it's also wonderful added onto mezze platters and served with things like roasted vegetables, My Favorite Hummus (page 147), Romesco Sauce (page 190), warm pita bread or flatbread, kalamata olives, pickled veggies, or even homemade or store-bought falafel.

Place the kale in a large bowl. Drizzle 1 tablespoon of the olive oil over the kale and massage thoroughly with your hands. Add the remaining 1 tablespoon olive oil, the chickpeas, quinoa, cucumber, bell pepper, tomatoes, parsley, red onion, mint, vinegar, and garlic to the bowl. Season with salt and pepper and toss lightly. Give it a taste and add more olive oil, red wine vinegar, salt, and black pepper, if needed, and serve.

Michelle's Tip

Make a small salad with the remaining cucumber, tomatoes, and onions, a small handful of fresh herbs, a dollop of mayonnaise or Greek yogurt, and a few splashes of vinegar.

Freestyle it

Substitutions for kale: baby arugula, baby kale, spinach

Substitutions for chickpeas: cannellini beans, fava beans, Great Northern beans, brown lentils, navy beans

Substitutions for quinoa: brown rice, bulgur wheat, couscous, farro, small pasta

SMOKED MOZZARELLA & SPINACH

Pasta Salad

Serves 4 to 6

If there's one pasta salad that is in heavy rotation in my kitchen, it is this one, inspired by a Whole Foods Market salad. It's slightly zingy, creamy, and there's just something about that smoked mozzarella that keeps everyone coming back for more, time and time again.

Cook the pasta: Bring a large pot of salted water to a rolling boil over high heat. Stir in the pasta and cook to tender according to the package directions. Meanwhile, put the spinach in a large colander and set it in the sink.

Once the pasta is tender, drain it into the colander over the spinach to wilt the spinach. Run cold water over the spinach and pasta and drain.

Make the pasta salad: Once cooled, transfer the pasta and spinach to a large bowl and add the smoked mozzarella, mayonnaise, roasted red bell pepper, parmesan, vinegar, cayenne, garlic, and basil. Season with salt and pepper. If the salad is too dry, add water 1 tablespoon at a time to moisten. Cover and refrigerate for 20 minutes to chill. Serve chilled.

Fine sea salt to taste

8 ounces (225 g) cavatappi, fusilli, or rotini pasta

4 cups (80 g) loosely packed baby spinach, roughly chopped (see Michelle's Tip)

8 ounces (225 g) smoked mozzarella cheese (such as Murray's), cut into ½-inch (5 cm) cubes

½ cup (112 g) mayonnaise

1 small jarred roasted red pepper, roughly chopped

3 tablespoons freshly grated parmesan cheese

2 tablespoons red wine vinegar

Pinch of cayenne pepper

1 garlic clove, grated

Small handful of fresh basil leaves, sliced into thin ribbons

Freshly ground black pepper to taste

Michelle's Tip

With any remaining spinach, make spinach and cheese quesadillas or cook the remaining 8 ounces of pasta and make a spinach pesto sauce to toss with it.

Saucy SOBA NOODLE SALAD

Serves 4

SAUCE

¼ cup (60 ml) tamari or soy sauce

1 tablespoon light brown sugar

1 tablespoon toasted sesame oil

1 tablespoon fresh lime juice

1 teaspoon grated fresh ginger

1 garlic clove, finely grated

TOFU

1 (14-ounce/397 g) package extra-firm tofu, drained

2 tablespoons tamari or soy sauce

Cooking oil spray

Fine sea salt to taste

VEGETABLES AND NOODLES

Fine sea salt to taste

1 medium broccoli crown, cut into bite-size florets (about 3 cups/210 g)

2 medium carrots, peeled into thin wide ribbons

4 ounces (115 g) soba noodles

1 medium avocado, thinly sliced

FOR SERVING (OPTIONAL)

Sliced scallions

Toasted sesame seeds

Freestyle it

Substitutions for brown sugar: agave nectar, honey, pure maple syrup

Substitutions for tofu: salmon, shrimp, tempeh

Substitutions for soba noodles: ramen noodles, rice noodles, udon noodles

Other additions to consider: asparagus, edamame, sugar snap peas, and snow peas. And in the colder months, roasted veggies are great with this as well.

I was first introduced to soba noodles after reading Heidi Swanson's cookbook *Super Natural Cooking* and quickly began adding them into my meal rotations after that. This salad is a riff on a recipe on the blog. It's the sort of thing I make when I'm craving a big bowl of noodle-y goodness with lots of fresh veggies. But I won't kid you, this salad is really all about the sauce. Those citrusy umami flavors work beautifully with these ingredients to bring it all together. Over the years many people have told me they don't really care for tofu because of its texture. Well, I find that when tofu first comes out of the oven or after frying it, it's still quite airy and light. But if you let it rest for a few minutes, the texture will become a little denser or firm, and that's how I've turned many people into tofu fans. This is delicious served either cold or warm, and I encourage you to play around with some of your favorite additions to the salad.

Preheat the oven to 400°F (200°C). Line a sheet pan with parchment paper.

Make the sauce: Combine the tamari, brown sugar, sesame oil, lime juice, ginger, and garlic in a large bowl and whisk until thoroughly incorporated. Set aside until ready to use.

Make the tofu: Press the tofu (see How to Press Tofu, page 18). Cut the pressed tofu into ¾-inch (2 cm) cubes or small triangles. Transfer to a plate or shallow dish and pour the tamari over the tofu. Flip each piece over so that the tamari coats all sides. Let the tofu marinate for 5 to 10 minutes.

Distribute the tofu evenly on the prepared sheet pan, mist the tofu lightly with cooking spray, and season lightly with salt. Bake for 30 minutes, flipping the tofu after 15 minutes. Set aside and let the baked tofu rest and cool for 5 minutes.

Make the vegetables and noodles: Set up a large bowl of ice and water. Fill a medium saucepan with salted water and bring to a boil over medium-high heat. Add the broccoli to the boiling water and blanch for about 1 minute. Add the carrot ribbons to the broccoli and bring back up to a boil. Continue cooking until the broccoli is bright green and crisp-tender, 2 to 3 more minutes. Once the vegetables are blanched, use a slotted spoon to transfer them to the ice bath to cool and then drain. Keep the pot of water at a boil.

Use the same saucepan of boiling water to cook the soba noodles according to the package directions, stirring occasionally. Once tender, drain the noodles and rinse with cold water.

Transfer the soba noodles, broccoli, and carrots to the large bowl with the sauce and toss lightly to coat. Put the noodle mixture on a serving platter or in a serving bowl along with the baked tofu and avocado. Garnish with the scallions and sesame seeds, if desired.

Easy
BLACK-EYED PEA SALAD

Serves 4

It's a shame that black-eyed peas really only have their time to shine on New Year's Day, when they're accompanied by a big pot of collard greens. Well, I'm changing things up a bit with this salad inspired by my friend Terra. She served it at a party once and I just couldn't stop thinking about it until I made this version. I consider it the distant cousin of the well-known salad Texas Caviar. It's perfect for potlucks, outdoor gatherings, or even road trips.

Combine the black-eyed peas, corn, bell pepper, red onion, parsley, garlic, vinegar, and olive oil in a large bowl. Season with salt and toss lightly. Give it a taste and add more vinegar, olive oil, or salt, if needed. (Now, wasn't that easy?!) Cover and refrigerate for 30 minutes so the flavors can marry. Serve chilled or at room temperature.

2 (15.5-ounce/439 g) cans black-eyed peas, drained and rinsed

1 cup (165 g) drained canned corn kernels

½ medium red bell pepper, finely diced

¼ cup (30 g) finely diced red onion

¼ cup (10 g) loosely packed flat-leaf parsley leaves, roughly chopped

1 garlic clove, minced

3 tablespoons unseasoned rice vinegar, plus more to taste

2 tablespoons extra-virgin olive oil, plus more to taste

Fine sea salt to taste

Freestyle it

Other additions to consider: cilantro instead of parsley, diced jalapeños, or diced tomatoes

Zesty Ranch
BROCCOLI-PASTA SALAD

Serves 4 to 6

Zesty Ranch Salad Dressing (recipe follows)

Fine sea salt to taste

8 ounces (225 g) conchiglie pasta (small shells) or fusilli

1 large broccoli crown, cut into bite-size pieces (about 5 cups/350 g)

1½ ounces (40 g) freshly grated parmesan cheese (about ½ cup), plus more to taste

Freshly ground black pepper to taste

I love mixing zesty Italian and ranch salad dressing together. And if you're not familiar with this combination, yep . . . it's totally a thing. When cooking the broccoli and pasta, I find it easier to use one pot and just blanch the broccoli when the pasta is almost cooked. To add a little more depth to the broccoli, roasting is another great option. Just let it cool before adding it into the salad.

Make Ahead Make the zesty ranch dressing as directed and refrigerate until serving.

Cook the pasta and broccoli: Bring a large pot of salted water to a boil over medium-high heat. Stir in the pasta and cook according to the package directions. Three minutes before the pasta is done, add the broccoli to the pot and bring back up to a boil. Continue cooking the pasta and broccoli until the pasta is tender and the broccoli is bright green and crisp-tender, about 3 minutes longer. Drain in a colander, run cold water over the pasta and broccoli, and drain once more. Set aside to cool.

Make the pasta salad: Combine the cooled pasta and broccoli, the parmesan, the desired amount of dressing (I usually start with ¾ cup and then add more as needed), and black pepper in a large bowl and toss to incorporate thoroughly. Give it a taste and add more dressing, salt, and pepper, if needed. Cover and refrigerate for 20 minutes so the flavors can marry. Serve chilled.

Freestyle it

Substitutions for broccoli:
asparagus, baby broccoli, fresh peas, Romanesco, or a combination of your favorite vegetables

Veganize it

Use vegan parmesan cheese and veganize the Zesty Ranch Dressing (recipe follows).

ZESTY RANCH DRESSING

Makes about 1¼ cups (300 ml)

½ cup (112 g) mayonnaise

½ cup (115 g) sour cream

2 tablespoons red wine vinegar or fresh lemon juice

1 tablespoon extra-virgin olive oil

1 teaspoon Italian seasoning

1 teaspoon dried minced onions

½ teaspoon Dijon mustard

½ teaspoon garlic powder

1 small garlic clove, peeled but whole

Pinch of cayenne pepper (optional)

Fine sea salt to taste

Combine the mayonnaise, sour cream, vinegar, olive oil, Italian seasoning, dried onions, mustard, garlic powder, garlic, cayenne, and salt in a small food processor or high-powered blender. Blend or process until smooth, about 30 seconds. Give it a taste and add more salt, if needed. Pour the dressing into a small airtight container and store in the refrigerator until ready to use. This dressing will keep in the refrigerator for up to 4 days. It may thicken with time; thin it with a little cool water, as needed.

Veganize it

Use vegan mayonnaise and vegan sour cream.

Buffalo Shrimp

SALAD

with Creamy Blue Cheese Dressing

Serves 2 to 4

When I stopped eating chicken years ago, I missed the slightly spicy and vinegary taste of Buffalo sauce that you typically find on hot wings. I started improvising by putting it on things like fried tofu and fried shrimp. And although you can certainly fry the shrimp if you prefer, I like to sauté them. They get slightly crispy, soak up the sauce, and become mouthwatering morsels that are finger-licking good! Whether you prefer creamy blue cheese or ranch dressing, I've got you covered by providing recipes for both.

Make Ahead Make your dressing of choice as directed in the recipe and refrigerate until serving.

Cook the Buffalo shrimp: Combine the shrimp, garlic powder, paprika, and salt and pepper in a medium bowl and stir to thoroughly coat the shrimp.

Heat the canola oil in a large nonstick or cast-iron skillet over medium heat. Add the shrimp, spaced evenly in the skillet. Cook undisturbed until they are golden and slightly crispy, 2 to 3 minutes per side. Add the hot sauce, butter, and honey. Stir to thoroughly coat the shrimp with the sauce. Season with a little more salt, if needed. Remove the skillet from the heat and let the shrimp cool slightly.

Assemble the salad: Arrange the romaine lettuce on a large platter or in a serving bowl. Top with the carrot, tomatoes, red cabbage, blue cheese, and celery. Give the Buffalo shrimp one more stir to be sure they are fully coated with the sauce and add them on as well. (Look at how beautiful and vibrant that is!)

Serve immediately with the dressing on the side so that everyone can drizzle several spoonful's onto their individual servings (there will be some dressing left over).

Veganize it

For the Buffalo sauce, use agave nectar instead of honey and nondairy butter. In place of the shrimp, use baked or fried tofu, crispy chickpeas, fried oyster mushrooms, plant-based chicken, or roasted cauliflower and toss in the Buffalo sauce per the instructions. For the salad, use a vegan salad dressing and replace the blue cheese with vegan feta cheese.

Creamy Blue Cheese Dressing or Ranch Dressing (recipes follow)

BUFFALO SHRIMP

1 pound large shrimp, peeled and deveined

½ teaspoon garlic powder

½ teaspoon paprika

Fine sea salt and freshly ground black pepper to taste

2 tablespoons canola oil

3 tablespoons Frank's RedHot hot sauce

1 tablespoon unsalted butter

Drizzle of honey

SALAD

1 large head romaine lettuce, roughly chopped (about 6 cups/330 g)

1 medium carrot, peeled and coarsely shredded (about ½ cup/55 g)

½ pint cherry tomatoes, halved (about 1 cup/145 g)

½ cup (50 g) thinly sliced red cabbage

2 ounces (55 g) blue cheese, crumbled

1 small celery stalk, thinly sliced

RECIPE CONTINUES →

CREAMY BLUE CHEESE DRESSING

Makes about 1½ cups (360 ml)

¾ cup (170 g) mayonnaise
½ cup (115 g) sour cream
2 ounces (55 g) blue cheese, crumbled (about ½ cup), or more to taste
¼ cup (60 ml) plus 2 tablespoons whole milk, or more as needed
1 teaspoon distilled white vinegar
½ teaspoon garlic powder
½ teaspoon Worcestershire sauce
½ teaspoon Dijon mustard
Fine sea salt and freshly ground black pepper to taste

Combine the mayonnaise, sour cream, blue cheese, milk, vinegar, garlic powder, Worcestershire sauce, mustard, salt, and black pepper in a small food processor or high-powered blender. Blend on high speed or process until smooth and creamy, about 30 seconds. If you prefer the dressing to be chunky, stir in 1 to 2 tablespoons more blue cheese after the dressing is blended. If the dressing is too thick, add milk, 1 tablespoon at a time, to thin to desired consistency. Give it a taste and add more salt, if needed. Pour the dressing into a small airtight container and store in the refrigerator until ready to use. This dressing will keep in the refrigerator for up to 1 week. It may thicken with time; thin it with a little cool water, as needed.

RANCH DRESSING

Makes about 1¼ cups (300 ml)

½ cup (112 g) mayonnaise
½ cup (115 g) sour cream
⅓ cup (80 ml) whole milk, or more to taste
2 teaspoons distilled white vinegar or dill pickle juice
1 teaspoon dried chives
½ teaspoon dried dill
½ teaspoon Italian seasoning
½ teaspoon garlic powder
¼ teaspoon onion powder
¼ teaspoon ground black pepper
Fine sea salt to taste

Combine the mayonnaise, sour cream, milk, vinegar, dried chives, dill, Italian seasoning, garlic powder, onion powder, black pepper, and salt in a small food processor or high-powered blender and blend or process until smooth and creamy, about 15 seconds. Pour the dressing into a small airtight container and store in the refrigerator until ready to use. This dressing will keep in the refrigerator for up to 1 week. It may thicken with time; thin it with a little cool water, as needed.

Veganize it

Use vegan mayonnaise, vegan sour cream, and unsweetened nondairy milk.

Grilled Tuna
SALAD
with Ginger-Sesame Dressing

Serves 2 to 4

My love for grilled tuna is fairly recent. One of Alex's friends grilled some lightly seasoned tuna steaks for us for dinner one night and I've been hooked ever since. For this, the tuna takes on some of the flavors from the marinade and then has this smoky flavor going on from the grill. And it's absolutely fabulous paired with the ginger-sesame dressing. For the wonton strips, I like to fry them up right before I fire up the grill so that Alex and I can have a few to snack on while the tuna is cooking. If you don't have time to make those, a substitute can easily be found in the salad topping section in most markets. I've also included instructions for how to make this indoors if you don't have access to an outdoor grill.

Prepare the tuna: Put the tuna fillets in a shallow dish. Pour the tamari and sesame oil over the tuna and turn to coat. Cover and marinate in the refrigerator for 20 minutes, flipping after 10 minutes.

To grill outdoors: Heat an outdoor grill to 425°F (220°C) or to medium-high heat. Brush the grill grates with the olive oil to prevent sticking. Lightly season the tuna fillets with salt and pepper. Transfer the tuna fillets to the grill and cook until browned and rare to medium-rare, 1 to 2 minutes on each side, or until medium-well to well done, 3 to 5 minutes on each side. The cook time will vary based on the thickness of the fillets. Keep in mind, the tuna will cook a bit more as it rests.

To pan-sear the tuna: Heat the olive oil in a large nonstick or cast-iron skillet over medium heat. Put the steaks in the skillet and sear until browned and rare to medium-rare, 1 to 2 minutes on each side, or until medium-well to well done, 3 to 5 minutes on each side. The cook time will vary based on the thickness of the fillets. Keep in mind, the tuna will cook a bit more as it rests.

Once the tuna fillets are cooked, transfer them to a plate to rest while you assemble the salad.

Ginger-Sesame Dressing (recipe follows)

GRILLED TUNA

2 yellowfin tuna fillets (6 ounces/ 170 g each)

2 tablespoons tamari or soy sauce

1 tablespoon toasted sesame oil

1 tablespoon olive or canola oil for the grill grates or skillet

Fine sea salt and freshly ground black pepper to taste

SALAD

1 large head romaine lettuce, roughly chopped (about 6 cups/330 g)

1 medium carrot, peeled and coarsely shredded (about ½ cup/55 g)

½ medium English cucumber, thinly sliced (about 1 cup/130 g)

1 to 2 cups crispy wonton strips (optional), store-bought or homemade (page 132)

2 scallions, thinly sliced

Black sesame seeds, for garnish

Veganize it

Omit the tuna and add grilled, baked, or pan-seared tofu or tempeh.

RECIPE CONTINUES →

Assemble the salad: Put the romaine lettuce in a large bowl. Top with the carrot, cucumber, and crispy wonton strips (if using) and give that a good toss. Divide among individual serving plates.

Using a chef's knife, slice the tuna into slices ½ inch (1.3 cm) thick. Top the salads with the tuna slices and sprinkle with the scallions and black sesame seeds. Drizzle with the ginger-sesame dressing. Serve any remaining dressing alongside.

GINGER-SESAME DRESSING

Makes about ½ cup (120 ml)

3 tablespoons unseasoned rice vinegar

2 tablespoons tamari or soy sauce

1 tablespoon extra-virgin olive oil

1 tablespoon toasted sesame oil

1 tablespoon honey

2 teaspoons grated fresh ginger

1 teaspoon toasted white sesame seeds

1 garlic clove, finely grated

Combine the vinegar, tamari, olive oil, sesame oil, honey, ginger, sesame seeds, and garlic in a small bowl and whisk until thoroughly incorporated. Store in the refrigerator until ready to use.

Veganize it

Use pure maple syrup or agave nectar instead of honey.

Deli

TUNA-PASTA SALAD

Serves 4

Alex and I often snack on things like pickles, olives, and cheese and crackers. And at any given time, if you open our refrigerator, you will find half-full jars of pickled things hanging out inside the door panel. Well, if you're anything like us, this salad is the perfect way to use up some of those jars that you might also have. Instead of the salami or prosciutto in your typical deli salad, I use tuna here as a delicious work-around. If you have a low tolerance for spice, consider using banana peppers instead of pepperoncini, or simply omit them.

Make the vinaigrette: Combine the olive oil, vinegar, Italian seasoning, garlic powder, salt, and black pepper in a large bowl and whisk to thoroughly incorporate. Set aside until the pasta is cooked.

Make the pasta salad: Bring a large pot of salted water to a rolling boil over high heat. Stir in the pasta and cook to tender according to the package directions. Drain and allow to cool completely. Transfer the pasta to the bowl with the vinaigrette and stir to evenly coat.

Add the tuna (keeping the tuna in bite-size pieces), arugula, pepperoncini, olives, provolone, roasted pepper, and parmesan to bowl with the pasta and lightly toss together. Give it a taste and season with salt and pepper, if needed. If the salad seems too dry, add a drizzle or two of olive oil and additional vinegar. Serve chilled.

VINAIGRETTE

⅓ cup (80 ml) extra-virgin olive oil, plus more as needed

¼ cup (60 ml) red wine vinegar, plus more as needed

½ teaspoon Italian seasoning

¼ teaspoon garlic powder

Fine sea salt and freshly ground black pepper to taste

PASTA SALAD

Fine sea salt to taste

8 ounces (225 g) fusilli or rotini pasta

2 (5-ounce/142 g) cans water-packed wild-caught chunk light tuna, drained

3 cups (60 g) lightly packed baby arugula

5 to 8 pepperoncini, stemmed, seeded, and sliced (about ⅓ cup/40 g)

½ cup (55 g) pitted green olives, such as Castelvetrano, halved

4 slices provolone cheese, sliced into thin strips

1 small roasted red bell pepper, from the jar or homemade (see Michelle's Tip), roughly chopped

3 tablespoons freshly grated parmesan cheese

Freshly ground black pepper

Michelle's Tip

To roast a red bell pepper, preheat the oven to 450°F (230°C). Cut off the top of the pepper, then halve it and remove the seeds and ribs. Place on a small sheet pan lined with foil. Roast until soft and slightly charred, 20 to 25 minutes. Allow to cool before peeling off the charred skin.

Veganize it

Omit the tuna and cheese; use vegan cheese slices and vegan parmesan cheese.

Freestyle it

Substitutions for tuna: cooked salmon, smoked trout

Other additions to consider: cannellini beans, chickpeas, hearts of palm, marinated artichoke hearts

SALMON-AVOCADO *Caprese-ish* SALAD

with Balsamic Glaze

Serves 2 to 4

I make this salad *a lot*—especially during the summer months when my homegrown tomatoes are in abundance. With the addition of fresh mozzarella and balsamic glaze, it gives me all the vibes of a traditional caprese salad, but not exactly. For this you can either make your own balsamic glaze, which is really simple, or you can use a store-bought product. Any leftover balsamic glaze can be drizzled over grilled or roasted vegetables or seafood, bruschetta, fresh fruit, pasta salads, or pizza (see The Panzanella-ish Pizza, page 138).

2 to 3 tablespoons balsamic glaze, store-bought or homemade (recipe follows)

SALMON

1 pound (450 g) skinless salmon fillet, cut into 2 portions

1 teaspoon Italian seasoning

½ teaspoon paprika

Fine sea salt and freshly ground black pepper to taste

1 tablespoon canola oil

SALAD

1 large head romaine lettuce, roughly chopped (about 6 cups/330 g)

1 medium avocado, sliced

½ pint cherry tomatoes or Sungold tomatoes, halved (about 1 cup/145 g)

1 cup (165 g) ciliegine mozzarella balls, halved

A small handful of fresh basil leaves (optional), torn

Fine sea salt and freshly ground black pepper to taste

Make Ahead Make the balsamic glaze as directed in the recipe and set aside.

Cook the salmon: Put the salmon fillets on a plate and pat dry with paper towels. Season the salmon on both sides with the Italian seasoning, paprika, and salt and pepper.

Heat the canola oil in a large nonstick or cast-iron skillet over medium heat. Once shimmering, add the salmon fillets, spacing them a couple inches apart. Cook until the salmon is opaque, golden, and crispy, 5 to 7 minutes on one side, depending on the thickness of the fillets. Carefully flip with a fish spatula and cook for an additional 3 to 4 minutes. Once the salmon is cooked through, carefully transfer the fillets to a plate and allow them to rest for a few minutes.

Assemble the salad: Arrange the romaine lettuce on a large platter. Top with the avocado, tomatoes, ciliegine, salmon, and fresh basil (if using). Season with salt and pepper and drizzle generously with the balsamic glaze. Serve immediately.

Freestyle it

Substitutions for salmon: halibut, scallops, shrimp, trout

Substitutions for romaine lettuce: butter lettuce, Little Gems, mixed field greens

Veganize it

Omit the salmon and cheese; use vegan mozzarella cheese and consider adding crispy tofu, pan-seared artichokes, or hearts of palm.

BALSAMIC GLAZE

Makes about ¼ cup (60 ml)

½ cup (120 ml) balsamic vinegar
2 tablespoons pure cane sugar or granulated sugar (optional)

Combine the balsamic vinegar and sugar (if using) in a small saucepan. Simmer over medium-low heat until the vinegar reduces by half and becomes syrupy, 10 to 15 minutes. (Keep in mind that the glaze will continue to thicken a bit as it cools.) Remove from the heat and cool completely. Pour into a small airtight container and store in the refrigerator until ready to use or for up to 2 weeks.

Soup
FOR THE SOUL

It may be a little unusual to some to crave soup year-round—not just in the colder months. But I admit that I make a pot of soup *at least* once a week—whether it's 30°F outside or 100°F. I mean . . . that's what the air conditioner is for, am I right? There's just something about soup that has the ability to speak to the soul and warm the heart. In this chapter, I've included my go-to Liquid Gold Vegetable Broth (page 68), along with twenty-six soup recipes. That's basically a soup for every other week of the year! And because I typically make soup based on my mood, I've divided this chapter into four sections: Feel Good Soups (when I need a pick-me-up), Got a Little Kick (when I'm craving something with a little spice), Comfy Cozy Soups (when I need a hug in the form of soup), and About That Chowder Life (when I'm craving something a little heartier or the catch of the day). I've also included recipes for some of my favorite soup (and salad) toppings (see Let's Top It!, pages 132–33).

Liquid Gold
VEGETABLE BROTH

Makes about 4 quarts (3.8 liters)

1 tablespoon extra-virgin olive oil

1 large yellow onion, unpeeled and halved lengthwise

2 medium celery stalks, cut into thirds

2 large carrots, cut into thirds

1 large bulb garlic, ¼ inch (6 mm) of the top trimmed off

1 medium leek, trimmed, halved, and fanned out to thoroughly rinse, then cut crosswise

2 ounces (55 g) dried porcini mushrooms

1 tablespoon fine sea salt, or to taste

1 teaspoon dried basil

1 teaspoon dried parsley

½ teaspoon ground turmeric

½ teaspoon black peppercorns (about 30 berries)

I don't always have time to make homemade vegetable broth, but when I do, the reward is this magical elixir that I call "liquid gold." I highly recommend using this broth when making soups like my Feel Better Chickpea Noodle Soup (page 73) and Vegetable Rice Soup (page 78), because it's the absolute perfect "no-chicken" type of vegetable broth. I use dried herbs for this broth, but a small handful of fresh herbs works just as well. When I don't have time to make my own broth, my favorite store-bought broth is the low-sodium Vegetarian No-Chicken Broth made by Imagine. Since most cartons of broth contain around 32 fluid ounces or 4 cups (950 ml), if the recipe calls for 5 cups (1.2 liters) broth, I see nothing wrong with adding 1 cup (240 ml) of water instead of buying two cartons of broth. You may need to adjust the amount of salt if you use broth plus water. This also applies when using Better Than Bouillon or bouillon cubes.

Heat the olive oil in an 8-quart (7.5-liter) stockpot or Dutch oven over medium heat. Place the onion halves (cut sides down) on one side of the pot. Add the celery and carrots to the other side of the pot. Sauté the celery and carrots for 4 to 5 minutes, not disturbing the onion. The bottoms of the onion halves will brown slightly, but don't let them burn. If they appear to be cooking too fast, reduce the heat.

Pour in 4 quarts plus 1 cup (17 cups/4 liters) water, then add the garlic bulb, leek, mushrooms, salt, basil, parsley, turmeric, and black peppercorns. Bring to a boil over medium-high heat, cover tightly, and reduce the heat to medium-low. Simmer for 1 hour. Remove from the heat, uncover, and allow the broth to cool completely.

Strain the broth through a large fine-mesh sieve into another large pot or bowl (compost or discard the solids). Transfer the broth to airtight storage bags or freezer-safe containers and store for up to 5 days in the refrigerator or up to 3 months in the freezer (see Michelle's Tip).

Michelle's Tip

When freezing, be sure to leave at least 2 inches (5 cm) at the top (called headspace) to allow for expansion. I know a lot of people prefer to not use plastic, but if you're like me with limited freezer space, consider storing the broth in freezer-safe storage bags or silicone bags such as Stasher bags or Souper Cubes. Fill the bags and tightly seal. Lay them flat on a sheet pan and place in the freezer. Once the broth has frozen, remove the sheet pans and store the bags flat.

Feel Good Soups

Feel Better
CHICKPEA NOODLE SOUP

Serves 4 to 6

Don't let the name of this soup fool you—you can enjoy it anytime, sniffles or not. I started making this soup as a work-around to the classic chicken noodle soup. Feel free to play around with the noodles you use: broken spaghetti noodles, egg noodles, and other pasta shapes work in this soup. Be sure to give it that squeeze of lemon at the end: It adds an unexpected but refreshing twist for the taste buds, which I love.

Heat the olive oil in a large pot or Dutch oven over medium-low heat. Add the carrots, celery, and onion and sauté until the onion has softened, about 5 minutes. Add the garlic and sauté until fragrant, about 1 minute. Stir in the vegetable broth, chickpeas, thyme, bay leaf, and turmeric. Season with salt and pepper. Cover the pot and simmer until the carrots are just tender, 5 to 7 minutes.

Uncover and increase the heat to medium-high. Stir in the pasta and cook, stirring occasionally, until al dente according to the package directions. Once the pasta is cooked, remove the pot from the heat (compost or discard the thyme sprigs and bay leaf). Stir in the lemon juice, taste, and add more juice, salt, and pepper, if needed.

Ladle the soup into individual bowls. If desired, serve with your favorite crackers. (Keep in mind that the noodles will continue to expand as the soup cools, so you may need to add a little more broth to second servings or leftovers.)

2 tablespoons extra-virgin olive oil

2 large carrots, peeled and thinly sliced

2 medium celery stalks, thinly sliced

1 medium yellow onion, roughly chopped

2 garlic cloves, minced

10 cups (2.4 liters) vegetable broth, store-bought or homemade (page 68)

1 (15-ounce/425 g) can chickpeas, drained and rinsed

4 fresh thyme sprigs

1 bay leaf

½ teaspoon ground turmeric

Fine sea salt and freshly ground black pepper to taste

6 ounces (170 g) rotini, fusilli, or spaghetti

Juice of 1 small lemon, or to taste

Crackers, for serving (optional)

Freestyle it

Substitutions for chickpeas: baked tofu, cannellini beans, Great Northern beans, jackfruit, navy beans, plant-based chicken

Other additions to consider: escarole, fresh parsley, fresh dill, kale, peas, spinach, Swiss chard, zucchini

Alphabet Soup
(FOR THE BIG KID IN YOU)

Serves 4 to 6

2 tablespoons extra-virgin olive oil

2 medium carrots, peeled and thinly sliced

1 medium yellow onion, finely diced

3 garlic cloves, minced

8 cups (1.9 liters) vegetable broth, store-bought or homemade (page 68)

2 medium russet potatoes, peeled and roughly chopped (about 2 cups/280 g)

2 cups (220 g) 2-inch (5 cm) pieces fresh green beans, or frozen or canned

1 teaspoon garlic powder

Fine sea salt and freshly ground black pepper to taste

1 cup (150 g) corn kernels, fresh, frozen, or canned

1 (14.5-ounce/411 g) can diced fire-roasted tomatoes with liquid

⅓ cup (56 g) alphabet pasta or other small pasta shape

One of the soups that I *always* looked forward to as a child was Mom's homemade vegetable beef soup with alphabet noodles. I would stand in my little yellow chair so that I would be tall enough to see her work her magic step-by-step—from what seemed to be such simple ingredients she would create this delicious pot of goodness. I think the best part was trying to find just the right letters so that I could spell out different words. Mom made it fun and this is an ode to her. Obviously, it doesn't include any beef, but every time I make it, I think of her.

I realize that not every market sells alphabet noodles, so feel free to substitute another small pasta shape such as stelline or orzo. Mom kept things really simple with this soup: It was old-fashioned with few spices or herbs. She let the vegetables speak for themselves. But if you want to add your own flare to it, such as fresh herbs, beans, or other seasonal vegetables, feel free to do so. And know that I'm sending you the biggest hug because Mom would have been so happy and proud. So be sure to take pictures of your versions of this soup—and/or your children's alphabet creations—and tag or share them with me!

Heat the olive oil in a large pot or Dutch oven over medium-low heat. Add the carrots and onion and sauté until the onion has softened, about 5 minutes. Add the garlic and sauté until fragrant, about 1 minute. Stir in the vegetable broth, potatoes, green beans, and garlic powder. Season with salt and pepper. Cover the pot and bring to a boil over medium heat. Simmer just until the potatoes begin to soften, 10 to 15 minutes.

Uncover and skim off and discard any foam on the surface of the soup. Increase the heat to medium-high and stir in the corn and tomatoes. Bring back up to a boil and stir in the pasta. Cover the pot and cook, stirring occasionally, until the pasta is al dente according to the package directions. Once the pasta is cooked, remove the pot from the heat. Uncover, taste, and add more salt and pepper, if needed.

Ladle the soup into individual bowls and serve. (Keep in mind that the noodles will continue to expand as the soup cools, so you may need to add a little more broth to second servings or leftovers.)

Sunshine DAL

Serves 4

I love adding lentils to soups and stews to make them a little heartier. And for this bowl of sunshine, I use red split lentils. I mean . . . we all could use a little sunshine in our lives, right?! Yesss! To brighten this up even more, I've added not only lemon juice but a little lemon zest as well. And let me tell ya, it's divine! I shared this soup with my neighbor Barbara and she said it's her "new favorite" soup and has made several requests for it, since then. I love to serve this with a dollop of sour cream or plain yogurt swirled in, along with warm naan, flatbread, or pita bread to help scoop up any remaining soup at the bottom of the bowl.

Heat the olive oil in a large pot or Dutch oven over medium-low heat. Add the carrots, potato, and onion and sauté until the vegetables begin to soften, 8 to 10 minutes. Add the garlic, turmeric, cumin, and coriander and sauté until fragrant, about 1 minute. Stir in the vegetable broth and lentils and season with salt. Cover the pot and simmer, stirring occasionally, until the carrots and potatoes are soft and the lentils are cooked through, 20 to 25 minutes.

If you're not wearing an apron, I highly recommend wearing one here, because I don't want you potentially staining your clothes during this step. Blend the soup with an immersion blender to the desired consistency, leaving some small chunks for texture. (Alternatively, let the soup cool slightly and then carefully transfer the soup to a high-powered blender. Blend until mostly smooth, leaving some small chunks for texture. If you need to work in batches, return the blended soup to the pot before continuing. Return all of the blended soup to the pot and rewarm over low heat, 2 to 3 minutes.)

Add more broth if the soup is too thick, then stir in the lemon zest and juice. Taste and adjust the salt, if needed. Ladle the soup into individual bowls and drizzle with olive oil. If desired, top with herbs and sour cream and serve with bread. (And if you have enough to share, ladle some of that in a to-go container for your neighbor; they'll thank you.)

3 tablespoons extra-virgin olive oil, plus more for drizzling

2 medium carrots, peeled and roughly chopped (about 1 cup/140 g)

1 medium russet potato, peeled and roughly chopped (about 1 cup/140 g)

1 medium yellow onion, finely diced

3 garlic cloves, minced

1 teaspoon ground turmeric

½ teaspoon ground cumin

½ teaspoon ground coriander

5½ cups (1.3 liters) vegetable broth, store-bought or homemade (page 68), plus more as needed

1¼ cups (250 g) red split lentils, picked through and rinsed

Fine sea salt to taste

Grated zest and juice of 1 medium lemon

FOR SERVING (OPTIONAL)

Chopped flat-leaf parsley leaves, dill leaves, or cilantro leaves

Dollop of sour cream or plain yogurt

Naan, flatbread, or pita bread

Freestyle it

Other additions to consider: a handful or two of kale, spinach, or Swiss chard (stirred in after the soup has been blended).

VEGETABLE RICE
Soup

Serves 4

2 tablespoons extra-virgin olive oil

3 medium carrots, peeled and thinly sliced

2 medium celery stalks, thinly sliced

1 medium yellow onion, finely diced

3 garlic cloves, minced

1 teaspoon Italian seasoning

9 cups (2.1 liters) vegetable broth, store-bought or homemade (page 68)

1 bay leaf

½ cup (92 g) long-grain white rice, rinsed

1 cup (150 g) corn kernels, fresh, frozen, or canned

1 small zucchini, roughly chopped (about 1 cup/115 g)

Fine sea salt and freshly ground black pepper to taste

Crackers, for serving (optional)

Another favorite soup growing up was Campbell's Chicken and Rice. All I needed was a handful of crackers to crumble in my bowl and I was truly a happy kid. This version foregoes the chicken, but still brings the same feel-good vibes. And if you're looking to switch things up a bit, add a squeeze of lemon or lime juice just before serving and a small handful of chopped fresh herbs like dill or parsley stirred in at the end, instead of the dried herbs.

Heat the olive oil in a large pot or Dutch oven over medium-low heat. Add the carrots, celery, and onion and sauté until the vegetables begin to soften, about 5 minutes. Add the garlic and Italian seasoning and sauté until fragrant, about 1 minute.

Stir in the vegetable broth and bay leaf. Bring to a boil over medium-high heat. Stir in the rice, corn, and zucchini. Season with salt and pepper. Cover the pot and simmer over medium-low heat until the rice is soft, 15 to 20 minutes. Stir occasionally, so the rice doesn't stick to the bottom of the pot.

Remove the pot from the heat (compost or discard the bay leaf). Give it a taste and add more salt and pepper, if needed. Ladle the soup into individual bowls. If desired, serve with your favorite crackers. (Keep in mind that the rice will continue to expand as the soup cools, so you may need to add a little more broth to second servings or leftovers.)

Freestyle it

Substitutions for rice: acini di pepe or another small pasta, cauliflower rice, pearl barley

MATZO BALL SOUP
Mash-Up

Serves 4

I fell in love with matzo ball soup when Mom and I would visit the Bagel Palace, a New York–style deli, years ago in Toco Hills. Unfortunately, they closed but gosh they had the best matzo ball soup. Well, this recipe is a mash-up of my love for both matzo ball soup and *caldo Xóchitl*, which I enjoyed back in my chicken-eating days. I know what you're thinking, but bear with me. See you have this no-chicken-y broth with these fluffy matzo balls, and then—like caldo Xóchitl (minus the shredded chicken)—enter the fresh components of tomatoes, sweet onions, jalapeño, cilantro, avocado, and a squeeze of lime juice. It's truly a chef's kiss, as they say. I realize some people prefer to cook matzo balls in a separate pot so the broth doesn't get cloudy . . . only adding them to the broth after they are cooked. In my opinion, they get more flavor from being cooked in the broth, but if you'd prefer, then do this: Reduce the amount of broth in the soup to 6 to 7 cups (1.4 to 1.7 liters). Bring a separate large pot of salted water to a boil and cook the matzo balls the same way as directed when you cook them in the broth. Once they are cooked, ladle them into the broth before serving.

Make the matzo balls: Whisk together the eggs, canola oil, and seltzer in a small bowl. Mix together the matzo meal, salt, and baking powder in a medium bowl. Pour the egg mixture into the matzo meal mixture and mix thoroughly. Cover and refrigerate for 30 minutes.

Make the soup: Heat the olive oil in a large pot or Dutch oven over medium-low heat. Add the celery, carrots, and onion and sauté until the vegetables begin to soften, about 5 minutes. Add the garlic and sauté until fragrant, about 1 minute. Stir in the vegetable broth and season with salt and pepper. Simmer until the carrots are just tender, 10 to 15 minutes.

When you're ready to make the matzo balls, run your hands under cold running water to dampen them. Use a small spoon and scoop the matzo ball mixture into your hands and roll the mixture to form a 1-inch ball. Use a light touch. Gently place the matzo balls into the soup as they are made and continue until all of the mixture is used. You will have about 8 matzo balls. If your hands get too dry or sticky, run your hands under cold water again. Cover the pot and simmer over medium-low heat for 30 minutes. Give the broth a taste and add more salt and pepper, if needed.

Ladle the matzo balls into individual bowls and add the broth and some vegetables. Garnish each bowl with several spoonfuls of pico de gallo, some avocado, cilantro, and a squeeze of lime.

MATZO BALLS
3 large eggs

3 tablespoons canola oil

3 tablespoons seltzer water or club soda

¾ cup (67 g) matzo meal

1 teaspoon fine sea salt

¼ teaspoon baking powder

SOUP
2 tablespoons extra-virgin olive oil

2 medium celery stalks, thinly sliced

2 medium carrots, peeled and thinly sliced

½ medium yellow onion, finely diced

2 garlic cloves, minced

8 cups (1.9 liters) vegetable broth, store-bought or homemade (page 68)

Fine sea salt and freshly ground black pepper to taste

FOR SERVING
Pico de Gallo (page 133)

Diced avocado

Chopped fresh cilantro

1 lime, quartered

Tomato & Corn
EGG DROP SOUP

Serves 4

2 tablespoons toasted sesame oil

½ medium yellow onion, thinly sliced

2 medium Roma or vine-ripened tomatoes, seeded and roughly chopped

4 cups (950 ml) vegetable broth, store-bought or homemade (page 68)

1 cup (150 g) corn kernels, fresh, frozen, or canned

2 tablespoons tamari or soy sauce, plus more to taste

¼ teaspoon ground white pepper, plus more to taste

Fine sea salt to taste

2 tablespoons arrowroot powder or cornstarch

2 large eggs

FOR SERVING

Sliced scallions

Crispy Wonton Strips (page 132)

Egg drop soup has been a favorite of mine since childhood—I would always order it when Mom and I had dinner at our favorite neighborhood Chinese restaurant. Believe it or not, I make this soup fairly often for breakfast and it was *very* close to being in What's for Brinner?! It takes just a short amount of time to cook and it's truly great any time of the day. I've added tomatoes and corn to my version, because they pair so well with eggs. Now, the crispy wonton strips are a must in my opinion. I always prepare a little extra, because anytime Alex sees me making them, he can't help but grab a handful to snack on.

Heat the sesame oil in a large pot or Dutch oven over medium-low heat. Add the onion and sauté until softened, about 3 minutes. Add the tomatoes and sauté just until warmed through, 1 to 2 minutes. Stir in the vegetable broth, corn, tamari, white pepper, and salt. Bring to a boil over medium-high heat, then reduce the heat to medium-low and simmer for 5 minutes. Skim off and discard any foam on the surface.

Make a slurry by whisking together the arrowroot powder and 3 tablespoons cold water in a small bowl. Quickly pour the slurry into the pot and immediately stir and incorporate it into the soup. The soup will thicken slightly.

Whisk the eggs in a separate small bowl. Slowly stir the soup in circles (like a small whirlpool) and drizzle the eggs into the center of the pot while stirring. Stop stirring as the eggs begin to form long ribbons. Remove the pot from the heat and let it sit for 5 minutes. Give it a taste and add more tamari, white pepper, or salt, if needed.

Ladle the soup into individual bowls and garnish with scallions. Serve the crispy wonton strips alongside.

Veganize it

Omit the eggs and consider using a handful of yuba sheets, thinly sliced.

Gingery Shrimp
& UDON NOODLE SOUP

Serves 4 to 6

This is definitely a pick-me-up soup. For the fragrant broth, I use ginger and a little bit of fish sauce, which adds another depth of flavor to it. Adjust the amount of ginger and fish sauce to your liking. I've always been a fan of the arts and I like to express myself creatively. So, this is a soup I like to take a little more time with presentation-wise . . . you know, make it all pretty-like.

Bring a medium saucepan of salted water to a boil over medium-high heat. Add the noodles, stir, and cook until tender according to the package directions. Drain and set them aside until the soup is ready.

Heat the sesame oil in a large pot or Dutch oven over medium-low heat. Add the carrots and ginger and sauté until the ginger is fragrant, about 1 minute. Stir in the vegetable broth, tamari, and fish sauce and bring to a boil over medium-high heat. Reduce the heat to medium-low and simmer until the carrots are tender, 8 to 10 minutes. Skim off and discard any foam on the surface. Taste the broth and add salt or more tamari or fish sauce, if needed.

Add the shrimp, bok choy, and snow peas to the pot. Simmer until the shrimp are fully cooked and the bok choy and snow peas are crisp-tender, 3 to 4 minutes. Remove the pot from the heat.

Use a pair of tongs to add udon noodles to individual bowls. Ladle over the broth, carefully arranging the vegetables and shrimp over the noodles (if it's easier to just ladle the vegetables and shrimp in, no big deal, it will still taste delish!). If desired, garnish with sliced scallions. Keep the bottles of tamari and fish sauce on the table in case anyone wants to add a drizzle or two to their bowls.

Fine sea salt to taste

6 ounces (173 g) dried udon noodles

1 tablespoon toasted sesame oil

2 medium carrots, peeled and cut into thin matchsticks (about 1 cup/110 g)

2 tablespoons grated fresh ginger

8 cups (1.9 liters) vegetable broth, store-bought or homemade (page 68)

2 tablespoons tamari or soy sauce, plus more for drizzling

1 tablespoon fish sauce, such as Red Boat, plus more for drizzling

12 ounces (340 g) large shrimp, peeled and deveined

4 baby bok choy, halved

1 cup (63 g) snow peas, trimmed and cut on a diagonal

Sliced scallions, for garnish (optional)

Freestyle it

Substitutions for udon noodles: frozen dumplings, ramen noodles, rice cakes, rice noodles, soba noodles, wontons, zoodles (zucchini noodles)

Other additions to consider: edamame, daikon, napa cabbage, puffed tofu, shiitake mushrooms, sugar snap peas, spinach, zucchini

Veganize it

Omit the fish sauce and use miso instead. Replace the shrimp with some of the suggestions in "Other additions to consider" (above) or use pan-seared or grilled tofu.

Got a
Little Kick

VEGETABLE & BLACK BEAN
Tortilla Soup

Serves 4

2 tablespoons canola oil

½ medium yellow onion, roughly chopped

4 garlic cloves, smashed

1 (14.5-ounce/411 g) can diced fire-roasted tomatoes with liquid

1 chipotle pepper in adobo sauce (see Michelle's Tip)

3 cups (710 ml) vegetable broth, store-bought or homemade (page 68), plus more as needed

1 small red bell pepper, roughly chopped

1 medium poblano pepper, seeded and finely diced

½ teaspoon ground cumin

½ teaspoon ground coriander

½ teaspoon chili powder

½ teaspoon dried oregano

1 (15-ounce/425 g) can black beans, drained and rinsed, or 1½ cups (277 g) home-cooked beans

1 cup (150 g) corn kernels, fresh, frozen, or canned

1 medium zucchini, roughly chopped

Fine sea salt to taste

FOR TOPPING (OPTIONAL)
Queso fresco or feta cheese

Diced avocado

Spiced Tortilla Strips (page 133) or store-bought tortilla chips/strips

1 lime, quartered

Chopped fresh cilantro

Sour cream or Mexican crema

I've been making a veggie variation of the classic tortilla soup for years. For the rich tomato broth, I like to use fire-roasted tomatoes. They lend to the smoky flavors as does the addition of a chipotle pepper, which gives it a little kick. And to make the soup heartier, I load it with veggies, black beans, and myriad toppings—which are all a must, in my opinion. They really bring this soup together to make it outrageously good.

Heat 1 tablespoon of the canola oil in a large pot or Dutch oven over medium heat. Add the onion and sauté just until softened, about 3 minutes. Add the garlic and sauté until fragrant, about 1 minute. Transfer the onion and garlic to a high-powered blender, along with the tomatoes, chipotle pepper, and 2 cups (480 ml) of the vegetable broth. Blend until smooth, about 30 seconds.

Using the same pot (no need to wash it), heat the remaining 1 tablespoon canola oil over medium heat. Add the red bell pepper and poblano pepper and sauté just until softened, 2 to 3 minutes. Add the cumin, coriander, chili powder, and oregano and sauté until fragrant, about 30 seconds. Stir in the blended tomato mixture, the black beans, corn, zucchini, and the remaining 1 cup (240 ml) vegetable broth. If you'd like a thinner broth, add another cup (240 ml) of vegetable broth. Season with salt. Cover the pot and simmer over medium-low heat until the zucchini has softened and the flavors meld, about 15 minutes, stirring occasionally. Give it a taste and add more salt, if needed.

Ladle the soup into individual bowls. Garnish with any or all of the toppings.

Michelle's Tip

Freeze any of the remaining chipotle peppers and adobo sauce in a small freezer-safe storage bag or container and use them in other recipes.

Freestyle it

Substitutions for the canned fire-roasted tomatoes: 3 medium Roma tomatoes, charred

Substitutions for the chipotle pepper in adobo: 1 to 2 dried chiles—such as ancho, morita, or guajillo—toasted, stemmed, seeded, and rehydrated

CURRY VEGETABLE
Ramen Soup

Serves 2 (with leftovers)

Can you say . . . flavor?! Well . . . this right here will take you straight to flavor town. Ramen noodle soup is constantly on rotation at our house, and I love to play around with not only the toppings but the broth as well. For this fragrant broth, I use curry powder and coconut milk, which really give the soup a soothing and nurturing vibe. You definitely won't be using the ramen seasoning packets here. As for the toppings, the possibilities are endless. Start with the ones I suggest, or use what you like. And if you prefer more broth than noodles, use only one package of ramen.

Cook the mushrooms and corn: Heat the canola oil in a medium saucepan over medium-high heat. Add the mushrooms and sauté until golden, 5 to 7 minutes. Season lightly with salt and pepper. Transfer the mushrooms to a plate. Add the corn to the pan and cook for several minutes, until heated through. Transfer the corn to the plate with the mushrooms.

Make the soup: In the same saucepan, heat the toasted sesame oil over medium-low heat. Add the onion and sauté just until softened, 3 to 5 minutes. Add the ginger, garlic, and curry powder and stir until fragrant, about 1 minute. Stir in the vegetable broth, coconut milk, and tamari and bring to a simmer. Once simmering, cook for 2 to 3 minutes to let the flavors meld. (Mmm . . . smells good, doesn't it!?) Give it a taste and add salt or more tamari, if needed.

Cook the carrots and noodles: Add 4 cups (950 ml) water to a separate medium saucepan if using one pack of ramen noodles; add 8 cups (1.9 liters) water if using two packs. Bring the water to a boil over medium-high heat and add the carrots. Cook the carrots for 2 to 3 minutes. With a slotted spoon, transfer the carrots to the plate with the mushrooms and corn. Skim any foam from the water. Keep the pot of water at a boil. Add the ramen noodles and cook according to the package directions. Once done, drain the noodles.

Ladle the broth into two bowls. Use tongs to divide the ramen noodles between the bowls and then top with the mushrooms, corn, and carrots. Garnish with any or all of the toppings.

2 tablespoons canola oil

8 ounces (225 g) cremini, shiitake, or white button mushrooms, thinly sliced

Fine sea salt and freshly ground black pepper

1 cup (150 g) corn kernels, fresh, frozen, or canned

1 teaspoon toasted sesame oil, plus more for drizzling

½ medium yellow onion, finely diced

1 teaspoon grated fresh ginger

1 garlic clove, grated

2 teaspoons mild yellow curry powder

5 cups (1.2 liters) vegetable broth, store-bought or homemade (page 68)

1 cup (240 ml) canned lite coconut milk

1 tablespoon tamari or soy sauce, plus more to taste

2 medium carrots, peeled and cut into matchsticks or shaved into thin ribbons

1 or 2 (4-ounce/115 g) packages ramen noodles, seasoning packets discarded

FOR TOPPING (OPTIONAL)
Soft-boiled eggs

Thinly sliced scallions

Chopped fresh cilantro

Hot chili oil or chili crisp

Michelle's Tip

For any leftover coconut milk, store in an airtight container in the refrigerator for up to 1 week or in the freezer for up to 6 months.

Freestyle it

Substitutions for ramen noodles: rice noodles, soba noodles, zoodles (zucchini noodles)

Creamy
ENCHILADA SOUP

Serves 4 to 6

2 tablespoons canola oil

1 medium yellow onion, roughly chopped

1 medium green bell pepper, roughly chopped

2 garlic cloves, minced

½ teaspoon ground cumin

½ teaspoon dried oregano

3 cups (710 ml) vegetable broth, store-bought or homemade (page 68)

1 (15-ounce/425 g) can black beans, drained and rinsed, or 1½ cups/277 g home-cooked beans

1 (14.5-ounce/411 g) can diced fire-roasted tomatoes with liquid

1 (10-ounce/283 g) can red enchilada sauce (about 1½ cups)

1 (4-ounce/113 g) can diced green chiles (optional)

Fine sea salt and freshly ground black pepper to taste

1 cup (150 g) corn kernels, fresh, frozen, or canned

1 small zucchini, roughly chopped

4 ounces (115 g) cream cheese

FOR TOPPING (OPTIONAL)

Chopped fresh cilantro

Tortilla chips or Spiced Tortilla Strips (page 133)

Sour cream

Shredded Monterey Jack or Mexican blend cheese

Sliced jalapeños

Veganize it

Omit the cream cheese or use vegan cream cheese.

If enchiladas and soup got together and had a baby, this would be it! I've seen a lot of variations of chicken enchilada soup, which ultimately brought me to this veggie version that can be personalized in many ways: Use pinto beans instead of black beans, throw in some kale or spinach, or you can even add a small scoop of rice to your bowl to make it even heartier. You get the picture.

Heat the canola oil in a large pot or Dutch oven over medium-low heat. Add the onion and bell pepper and sauté just until the vegetables begin to soften, 3 to 5 minutes. Add the garlic, cumin, and oregano and sauté until fragrant, about 1 minute.

Stir in the vegetable broth, black beans, tomatoes, red enchilada sauce, and green chiles (if using). Season with salt and pepper. Cover the pot and let simmer over medium heat for 10 minutes, stirring occasionally, to let the flavors meld.

Uncover and reduce the heat to medium-low. Add the corn, zucchini, and cream cheese and stir until the cream cheese is melted. Cover the pot and simmer just until the zucchini softens, 8 to 10 more minutes. Give it a taste and add more salt and pepper, if needed, and remove from the heat.

Ladle the soup into individual bowls. Garnish with any or all of the toppings.

Red Curry
COCONUT SOUP

Serves 6

This is inspired by a coconut soup served at one of my favorite Thai restaurants in Atlanta. It is fairly easy to make, and the stars of the show are the mushrooms, tofu, and broth. Once you've got that flavorful broth right, everything else falls into place. To make this soup a bit heartier, I occasionally serve it over rice noodles or sometimes even rice. And don't forget the lime, which adds that zing that y'all know I love.

Heat the canola oil in a large pot or Dutch oven over medium-low heat. Add the onion and sauté until softened, about 5 minutes. Stir in the red curry paste and ginger and sauté until fragrant, about 1 minute.

Stir in the vegetable broth, tamari, brown sugar, and lemongrass. Cover the pot and simmer for 10 minutes to let the flavors meld. Uncover and stir in the coconut milk, mushrooms, tofu, juice from the ½ lime, and the fish sauce (if using). Simmer, uncovered, until the mushrooms are tender, about 5 minutes. Give it a taste and add more tamari or fish sauce, if needed. Remove the soup from the heat (compost or discard the lemongrass).

Ladle the soup into individual bowls. Serve with lime wedges and cilantro. Keep the bottles of tamari and fish sauce on the table in case guests want to add a drizzle or two to their bowls.

1 tablespoon canola oil or coconut oil

½ medium yellow onion, thinly sliced

2 to 3 tablespoons Thai red curry paste (depending on how spicy you want it)

1 tablespoon grated fresh ginger

6 cups (1.4 liters) vegetable broth, store-bought or homemade (page 68)

3 tablespoons tamari or soy sauce, plus more for drizzling

1 to 2 tablespoons light brown sugar (depending on how sweet you want it)

1 lemongrass stalk, cut into two 4-inch (10 cm) pieces and smacked hard with the flat side of a chef's knife

1 (13.5-ounce/400 ml) can unsweetened coconut milk

8 ounces (225 g) shiitake, white button, or cremini mushrooms, thinly sliced

1 (14-ounce/397 g) package firm tofu, drained and cut into ½-inch (1.3 cm) cubes

½ medium lime, plus lime wedges for garnish

1 tablespoon fish sauce (optional), such as Red Boat, plus more to taste

Fresh cilantro leaves, for serving

Veganize it

Be sure to check the label on the red curry paste that you choose to ensure that it's vegan. There are a few companies that make vegan fish sauce, and you can even find recipes online if you search for it; if those are not accessible, simply omit the fish sauce and add a little more tamari or salt for that added umami flavor.

Freestyle it

Substitutions for tofu: shrimp

Hearty
VEGETARIAN CHILI

Serves 4

3 tablespoons canola oil

12 ounces (340 g) plant-based ground beef, such as Impossible Foods

1 medium yellow onion, finely diced

1 small green bell pepper, finely diced

2 teaspoons chili powder

1 teaspoon smoked paprika

½ teaspoon ground coriander

½ teaspoon dried oregano

¼ teaspoon ground cumin

3 tablespoons tomato paste

2 cups (480 ml) vegetable broth, store-bought or homemade (page 68)

1 (16-ounce/450 g) can chili beans (pinto) with mild chili sauce

1 (14.5-ounce/411 g) can petite-diced tomatoes with liquid

Fine sea salt and freshly ground black pepper to taste

FOR TOPPING (OPTIONAL)

Shredded cheddar cheese

Sliced jalapeños

Diced red onion

Sour cream

Spiced Tortilla Strips (page 133) or store-bought tortilla chips

I just didn't feel this chapter would be complete without including my hearty vegetarian chili. For this recipe I like to add plant-based ground beef, but you can use black beans or kidney beans instead. Add in seasonal vegetables as well, such as corn (summer) or leftover roasted sweet potatoes or butternut squash (fall). What I serve this chili with typically depends on my mood. When it's cold out, I like to eat it with Buttermilk Corn Bread (page 123) and in warmer months, I usually go with crackers or tortilla chips. And if you have any leftover chili, ladle some over a bed of French fries or Fritos for a fun meal.

Heat the canola oil in a large pot or Dutch oven over medium heat. Add the plant-based ground beef and sauté until slightly browned, about 5 minutes. Add the onion and bell pepper and sauté until the vegetables begin to soften, about 5 minutes. Stir in the chili powder, smoked paprika, coriander, oregano, cumin, and tomato paste and sauté until fragrant, about 1 minute.

Stir in the vegetable broth, chili beans, and tomatoes. Season with salt and pepper. Cover the pot and simmer over medium-low heat to let the flavors meld, 15 to 20 minutes. Uncover, taste, and add more salt and pepper, if needed.

Ladle the chili into individual bowls. Garnish with any or all of the toppings.

Freestyle it

Substitutions for plant-based ground beef: Stir in a 15-ounce (425 g) can drained and rinsed lentils, kidney beans, or black beans when you add the chili pinto beans. A few other substitutes: 8 ounces (225 g) roughly chopped mushrooms, sautéed until golden brown. Or a package of drained and pressed tofu, crumbled and sautéed until golden and crispy.

SHRIMP & OKRA
Gumbo

Serves 4 to 6

Now, I'll be the first to tell you that I'm no gumbo aficionado, but *this* Creole-inspired gumbo is one of my favorites to make. I watched Justin Wilson, a well-known Louisiana chef, on PBS growing up and as he cooked, he would often say "I gha-rawn-tee!" (I guarantee!). That just tickled me and I loved to watch him make gumbo, among other things. Now, if you've never made gumbo before, it is surely the kind of meal that you make when you have time to spare and a little bit of patience. Making a roux can be considered a labor of love, in my opinion, but it's totally worth it in the end.

Put on some nice music or your favorite playlist.

Make the roux: Heat the canola oil in a large pot or Dutch oven over medium-low heat. Once shimmering, stir in the flour. Continue to stir every couple of minutes for 30 to 40 minutes. The roux will go from a light beige color to brown and then to a dark brown color (like chocolate). The roux will also smell slightly nutty as it cooks. Be sure to watch it so that it does not burn. Reduce the heat to low if your roux seems to be browning too fast. (If at any time it smells burned, you will need to start over. And we don't want that.)

Meanwhile, be sure to take some breaks and do a little dancing in between.

Make the gumbo: Add the celery, bell pepper, and onion (known as the "holy trinity") and sauté, stirring occasionally, until the vegetables begin to soften, 8 to 10 minutes. Add the garlic, smoked paprika, thyme, black pepper, and cayenne. Sauté until fragrant and thoroughly incorporated with the vegetables, about 1 minute. Stir in the broth, tomatoes, okra, Worcestershire sauce, and bay leaves, and season with salt.

Cover the pot and simmer, stirring occasionally, until the okra is tender enough to break easily with the back of a spoon, 35 to 40 minutes.

Uncover and stir in the shrimp, then cover and simmer until the shrimp are fully cooked, about 5 more minutes. Give it a taste and add more salt, if needed. Remove the pot from the heat (compost or discard the bay leaves).

Ladle the gumbo into individual bowls. If desired, add rice and a sprinkle of parsley. (Eat good! You did that!)

½ cup (120 ml) canola oil

½ cup (63 g) all-purpose flour

2 medium celery stalks, finely diced

1 medium green bell pepper, finely diced

1 medium yellow onion, finely diced

4 garlic cloves, minced

1 teaspoon smoked paprika

½ teaspoon dried thyme

½ teaspoon ground black pepper

¼ teaspoon cayenne pepper

4 cups (950 ml) seafood broth or vegetable broth, store-bought or homemade (page 68)

1 (14.5-ounce/411 g) can diced tomatoes, drained well

8 ounces (225 g) fresh or frozen okra, cut crosswise into about ¾-inch (2 cm) lengths

A few dashes of Worcestershire sauce

2 bay leaves

Fine sea salt to taste

1 pound (455 g) large shrimp, peeled and deveined

FOR SERVING (OPTIONAL)
Cooked Long-Grain White Rice (page 179) or Brown Rice (page 178)

Chopped fresh flat-leaf parsley leaves

Veganize it

Use vegetable broth instead of the seafood broth and vegan Worcestershire sauce. Omit the shrimp and replace it with mushrooms and sliced plant-based Italian sausage that have been sautéed in a little oil in a large skillet until golden.

Freestyle it

Other additions to consider: crabmeat, crawfish, oysters, red snapper

Comfy Cozy Soups

Butternut Squash SOUP

with Halloumi Croutons

Serves 4 to 6

3 tablespoons extra-virgin olive oil

3 pounds butternut squash, peeled, halved, seeded, and cut into ¾-inch (2 cm) cubes

1 small yellow onion, roughly chopped

1 medium carrot, peeled and roughly chopped

3 garlic cloves, minced

4 cups (950 ml) vegetable broth, store-bought or homemade (page 68), plus more as needed

1 medium apple, such as Gala or Fuji, unpeeled, cored and roughly chopped

3 fresh thyme sprigs

Fine sea salt to taste

½ cup (120 ml) canned unsweetened coconut milk or half-and-half, plus more as needed

½ teaspoon ground ginger

2 tablespoons pure maple syrup

Pinch of ground cinnamon

Pinch of ground nutmeg

Halloumi Croutons (page 132)

This is by far one of my favorite soups to make when the leaves start to turn those beautiful autumn colors. It is like fall in a bowl. It's so rich and velvety, and the subtle hints of ginger, nutmeg, and cinnamon are *everything*. Another variation of warm spices that I enjoy using are ground cumin, coriander, and turmeric. To offset the natural sweetness of this soup, I serve it topped with Halloumi croutons. They will be *extremely* hard not to snack on while the soup cooks. Trust me.

Heat the olive oil in a large pot or Dutch oven over medium-low heat. Add the butternut squash, onion, and carrot and sauté just until the vegetables begin to soften, about 10 minutes. Add the garlic and sauté until fragrant, about 1 minute. Stir in the vegetable broth, apple, thyme sprigs, and salt. Cover the pot and simmer over medium heat, stirring occasionally, until the butternut squash is fork-tender, 20 to 25 minutes.

Uncover the soup (compost or discard the thyme sprigs). Allow the soup to cool slightly and then carefully ladle it into a high-powered blender. Blend until smooth. (If you need to blend in batches, return the blended portion of the soup to the pot before continuing.)

Pour all of the soup into the pot and stir in the coconut milk, ginger, maple syrup, cinnamon, and nutmeg. Simmer the soup over low heat for 5 minutes to rewarm and let the flavors meld. Adjust the consistency of the soup. If you'd like a creamier consistency, add a bit more coconut milk; if the consistency is too thick, add more vegetable broth. Give it a taste and add more salt, maple syrup, cinnamon, or nutmeg, if needed.

Ladle the soup into individual bowls and top with the Halloumi croutons.

Freestyle it

Substitutions for butternut squash: carnival squash, carrots, kabocha squash, pumpkin

Veganize it

Omit the Halloumi croutons.

Vegetarian ZUPPA TOSCANA

Serves 4 to 6

I posted this recipe on my blog several years ago and then shared an image of it on Instagram. Shortly after, my friends at Food52 reshared my creation. Not long after that, I got tagged by actress Jenna Fischer, who was making this soup and sharing her take on it in real-time with her Instagram community. I tell ya . . . Jenna almost broke the Internet that day, and since then, this has become the most popular soup on my blog. (Thanks, Jenna!) It's essentially my take on the popular Zuppa Toscana served at Olive Garden, but done a little differently.

Heat 2 tablespoons of the olive oil in a large pot or Dutch oven over medium-low heat. Add the plant-based ground sausage and sauté until the sausage is golden brown and slightly crispy, 10 to 15 minutes. Transfer the sausage to a bowl, cover, and set aside. (I prefer to add the plant-based sausage at the very end of the cooking process because it has the potential to lose its firmness if it's cooked too long in the broth.)

Using the same pot (no need to wash it), heat the remaining 1 tablespoon olive oil (or more, if needed) over medium heat. Add the onion and sauté until softened, about 5 minutes. Add the garlic, Italian seasoning, sun-dried tomatoes, and chile flakes and sauté until fragrant, about 1 minute. Pour in the wine and scrape the bottom of the pan to deglaze it. Sauté for a few minutes to let the alcohol cook off.

Stir in the vegetable broth and potatoes. Season with salt and pepper. Cover the pot and simmer over medium-low heat until the potatoes are fork-tender, 20 to 25 minutes.

Uncover, reduce the heat to low, and return the browned plant-based sausage to the pot with the kale and half-and-half. Stir to combine, then simmer until the kale wilts and the sausage is warmed through, about 5 more minutes. Taste, add more salt and pepper, if needed, and remove the soup from the heat.

Ladle the soup into individual bowls and serve with parmesan and crusty bread, if desired.

3 tablespoons extra-virgin olive oil, plus more as needed

14 ounces (400 g) plant-based ground sausage (1½ to 2 cups), such as Impossible Foods

1 medium yellow onion, roughly chopped

3 garlic cloves, minced

2 teaspoons Italian seasoning

2 tablespoons roughly chopped drained oil-packed sun-dried tomatoes

Pinch of red chile flakes

¼ cup (60 ml) dry white wine

6 cups (1.4 liters) vegetable broth, store-bought or homemade (page 68)

2 medium Yukon Gold potatoes, roughly chopped (about 2½ cups/350 g)

Fine sea salt and freshly ground black pepper to taste

3 cups (195 g) packed stemmed and thinly sliced lacinato or curly kale

1½ cups (360 ml) half-and-half

FOR SERVING (OPTIONAL)
Freshly grated parmesan cheese

Crusty artisan bread

Freestyle it

Substitutions for plant-based ground sausage: Stir in a 14.5-ounce (411 g) can drained and rinsed cannellini beans or Great Northern beans, or 1½ cups/277 g home-cooked beans when you add the potatoes, which will make it more of a Tuscan white bean soup.

Substitutions for kale: escarole, spinach, Swiss chard

Substitutions for potatoes: cauliflower, pasta, gnocchi

Veganize it

Use vegan wine or vegetable broth for deglazing, unsweetened nondairy creamer for the half-and-half, and vegan parmesan cheese.

CREAM OF ASPARAGUS *Soup*
with Herby Croutons

Serves 3 to 4

4 tablespoons (60 g) unsalted butter

1 pound (450 g) asparagus, cut into ½-inch (1.3 cm) pieces

½ medium yellow onion, finely diced

2 garlic cloves, minced

3 tablespoons all-purpose flour

4 cups (950 ml) vegetable broth, store-bought or homemade (page 68)

Fine sea salt and freshly ground black pepper to taste

¾ cup heavy cream (175 ml) or half-and-half (for a slightly lighter version)

Herby Croutons (page 133)

Believe it or not, this was one of Mom's favorite soups. When I was growing up, we'd typically have it on "soup and sandwich night" during the week. I wanted to include a recipe like this, because you can basically use this as a starting point for many "cream of fill-in-the-blank" soups, such as cream of mushroom, onion, celery, and so on. Switch out the asparagus and adjust the seasoning based on the vegetable you're using. For a little texture I like the addition of these herby croutons. They're great on soup as well as tossed in with salads.

Melt the butter in a large pot or Dutch oven over medium-low heat. Add the asparagus and onion and sauté until the onion has softened, about 5 minutes. Add the garlic and sauté until fragrant, about 1 minute. Sprinkle in the flour and stir continuously until it is thoroughly incorporated with the vegetables and turns slightly golden, 1 to 2 minutes. Stir in the vegetable broth and season with salt and pepper. Cover the pot and simmer over medium-low heat, stirring occasionally, until the thickest asparagus stalks are fork-tender and no longer fibrous, 20 to 25 minutes.

Uncover and blend the soup with an immersion blender to the desired consistency, leaving some small pieces for texture. (Alternatively, let the soup cool slightly and then carefully transfer to a high-powered blender. Blend until mostly smooth with some small pieces for texture. If you need to blend in batches, return the blended portion of the soup to the pot before continuing. Return all of the blended soup to the pot.)

Stir in the heavy cream and simmer for just a few more minutes, until heated through. Give it a taste and add more salt and pepper, if needed.

Ladle the soup into individual bowls and top with herby croutons.

Michelle's Tip

Cashew cream is often used as a dairy-free option for half-and-half or lite coconut milk; or with a higher proportion of cashews to water, it is a substitute for heavy cream or full-fat coconut milk. It's obviously not milk but it does add a creamy texture and look to whatever you're adding it to. For my cashew "half-and-half" (makes 1 scant cup/220 ml): Soak ⅓ cup (40 g) raw cashews in ⅔ cup (160 ml) warm water for 1 hour and then blend the cashews and water in a high-powered blender until completely smooth, about 30 seconds. For my cashew "heavy cream" (makes ¾ cup/175 ml): Soak ½ cup (60 g) raw cashews in ½ cup (120 ml) warm water for 1 hour and then blend the cashews and water in a high-powered blender until completely smooth, about 30 seconds. Alternatively, you can swap out the water (used for blending) for unsweetened and unflavored plant-based milk if you'd like. Pour the cashew cream into an airtight container and store in the refrigerator for up to 4 days.

Veganize it

Omit the butter and use a neutral oil or a nondairy butter. Use an unsweetened nondairy creamer for the heavy cream.

Comforting
BROCCOLI-CHEDDAR SOUP

Serves 3 to 4

I remember going to Panera Bread Company years ago, with the intention of ordering their broccoli-cheddar soup, only to be disappointed when I learned they cook their soup with chicken broth. So, I started making my own version at home, and it is a soup that I turn to often if I need a big bowl of comfort. When selecting the cheddar cheese to use, be sure to pick up a good-quality sharp cheddar cheese and grate it yourself. It will yield better results than preshredded cheese, which is typically coated with an anticaking agent. This is by far the thickest and creamiest soup in this chapter. If you prefer a slightly lighter version, increase the vegetable broth to 3½ cups (830 ml) and reduce the half-and-half to 1 cup (240 ml).

Melt the butter in a large pot or Dutch oven over medium-low heat. Add the onion and sauté until softened, about 5 minutes. Sprinkle in the flour and stir continuously until it is thoroughly incorporated with the onion and turns slightly golden, 1 to 2 minutes. Slowly stir in the vegetable broth and continue stirring until thoroughly mixed and lump-free. Stir in the half-and-half, broccoli, carrot, and garlic powder. Cover the pot and simmer over low heat, stirring occasionally, until the broccoli is crisp-tender, about 15 minutes.

Uncover and blend the soup with an immersion blender to the desired consistency, leaving some small broccoli florets for texture. (Alternatively, let the soup cool slightly and then carefully transfer to a high-powered blender. Blend until mostly smooth, leaving some small broccoli florets for texture. Return the blended soup to the pot. If you need to blend in batches, return the blended portion of the soup to the pot before continuing.)

Stir in the cheddar and simmer over low heat until the cheese is completely melted and warmed through, 2 to 3 minutes. Give it a taste and season with salt and pepper.

Ladle the soup into individual bowls and serve with a warm baguette. (Mmmm . . . comfort!)

4 tablespoons (60 g) unsalted butter

½ medium yellow onion, finely diced

¼ cup (31 g) all-purpose flour

2½ cups (590 ml) vegetable broth, store-bought or homemade (page 68), plus more as needed

2 cups (480 ml) half-and-half

1 large broccoli crown, cut into bite-size pieces (about 5 cups/350 g)

1 medium carrot, peeled and coarsely shredded (about ½ cup/55 g)

½ teaspoon garlic powder

5 ounces (140 g) coarsely grated sharp cheddar cheese (about 2 cups)

Fine sea salt and freshly ground black pepper to taste

Baguette, warmed, for serving

Veganize it

Use a neutral oil or a nondairy butter, unsweetened nondairy creamer for the half-and-half, and meltable vegan cheese shreds and/or nutritional yeast for the cheddar.

Michelle's Tip

To make grating cheese a little easier, place the cheese in the freezer for 10 to 15 minutes. Or mist your grater with a little cooking spray right before grating. This will help the cheese glide better and prevent it from sticking as much.

Hearty
CABBAGE & LENTIL SOUP

Serves 6

2 tablespoons extra-virgin olive oil

2 medium carrots, peeled and roughly chopped

1 medium yellow onion, roughly chopped

1 medium green bell pepper, roughly chopped

½ medium head green cabbage, thinly sliced (about 4 cups/380 g)

4 garlic cloves, minced

1 teaspoon Italian seasoning

7 cups (1.7 liters) vegetable broth, store-bought or homemade (page 68)

1 (14.5-ounce/411 g) can diced fire-roasted tomatoes with liquid

½ cup (95 g) green lentils or brown lentils, picked through and rinsed

1 teaspoon garlic powder

½ teaspoon smoked paprika

1 bay leaf

Fine sea salt and freshly ground black pepper to taste

I like to think of this soup as a veggie version of a stuffed cabbage soup, but here I use lentils instead of beef. Although this soup is hearty, I always find myself adding a small spoonful of cooked rice to my bowl in the colder months, which really turns it into a meal in a bowl.

Heat the olive oil in a large pot or Dutch oven over medium-low heat. Add the carrots, onion, bell pepper, and cabbage and sauté until the vegetables begin to soften, about 5 minutes. Add the garlic and Italian seasoning and sauté until fragrant, about 1 minute.

Stir in the vegetable broth, tomatoes, lentils, garlic powder, smoked paprika, and bay leaf. Season with salt and pepper. Cover the pot and simmer over medium heat, stirring occasionally, until the lentils and cabbage are both tender, about 20 minutes (for green lentils) and 25 to 30 minutes (for brown lentils). Remove from the heat and uncover (compost or discard the bay leaf). Give it a taste and add more salt and pepper, if needed.

Ladle the soup into individual bowls and serve.

Michelle's Tip

To use the leftover half head of cabbage: Sauté thinly sliced cabbage with onions, bell peppers, and plant-based Italian sausage. Or cut in half, roast or braise the quarters, and serve them as an accompaniment to an entrée.

Vegetarian
FRENCH ONION SOUP

Serves 4 to 6

I love this soup. But I usually can't order it when dining out because it's typically prepared with beef broth. So, I've solved that problem simply by using vegetable broth. The end result may not be as dark as the traditional beef broth version, but it's just as rich and delicious, especially with my additions of tamari and Worcestershire sauce, which help to deepen the umami flavor.

Make the soup: Melt the butter in a large pot or Dutch oven over medium heat. Add the onions and season liberally with salt. Stir to separate the onion rings. Cover the pot and let the onions cook down and soften, stirring occasionally, 8 to 10 minutes.

Uncover the pot and cook until the onions turn a caramel color, stirring often to prevent burning. This can take 30 to 45 minutes. (Yes . . . I know! So, be sure to take a few dance breaks while you're stirring!) If the pot gets too dry, stir in 1 or 2 tablespoons water.

Pour in the dry sherry to deglaze the pot, stirring well for 2 to 3 minutes to loosen any browned bits from the bottom of the pot and to cook off most of the sherry. Stir in the vegetable broth, tamari, Worcestershire sauce, thyme sprigs, and bay leaf. Season with salt and pepper. Cover the pot and simmer over low heat to let the flavors meld, about 15 minutes. Give it a taste and add more tamari or salt, if needed. Remove the pot from the heat (compost or discard the thyme sprigs and bay leaf).

Make the Gruyère toast: Preheat the oven to 425°F (220°C).

Arrange the baguette slices on a sheet pan and drizzle each side lightly with olive oil. Bake until lightly toasted, about 8 minutes. Remove from the oven and sprinkle each slice liberally with the Gruyère. Turn the broiler to high and broil the toasts until the cheese is melted and bubbling, 1 to 2 minutes.

Ladle the soup into individual bowls, place 1 or 2 Gruyère toasts into each bowl, and serve.

SOUP

4 tablespoons (60 g) unsalted butter

3 pounds (1.4 kg) sweet onions, such as Vidalia, thinly sliced

Fine sea salt to taste

¼ cup (60 ml) dry sherry

6 cups (1.4 liters) vegetable broth, store-bought or homemade (page 68)

1 tablespoon tamari, or more if needed

1 teaspoon Worcestershire sauce

4 fresh thyme sprigs

1 bay leaf

Freshly ground black pepper to taste

GRUYÈRE TOAST

1 baguette, cut into ½-inch (1.3 cm) slices (1 or 2 slices per serving, depending on the width of the baguette)

Extra-virgin olive oil

4 ounces (115 g) Gruyère cheese, grated (1 heaping cup)

Veganize it

Use nondairy butter, vegan wine or vegetable broth for deglazing, vegan Worcestershire sauce or miso paste, and meltable vegan mozzarella cheese shreds.

CHUNKY TOMATO & CHEESE
Tortellini Soup

Serves 6

2 tablespoons extra-virgin olive oil

1 large carrot, peeled and finely diced

1 medium celery stalk, finely diced

1 small yellow onion, finely diced

3 garlic cloves, minced

2 teaspoons Italian seasoning

Pinch of red chile flakes

5 cups (1.2 liters) vegetable broth, store-bought or homemade (page 68)

1 (14.5-ounce/411 g) can petite-diced tomatoes with liquid

1 (14.5-ounce/411 g) can crushed tomatoes

½ teaspoon garlic powder

Fine sea salt and freshly ground black pepper to taste

1 (9- or 10-ounce/255 or 283 g) package fresh cheese tortellini

3 cups (60 g) loosely packed baby spinach, roughly chopped

1 cup (240 ml) heavy cream

FOR SERVING (OPTIONAL)
Freshly grated parmesan cheese

Freshly torn basil leaves

Baguette, warmed

This recipe is a Supper with Michelle blog favorite. The creamy tomato base and those tender cheese tortellini are so craveable. This soup is loaded with vegetables and you can swap out the carrots and spinach for a little bit of butternut squash and kale or Swiss chard during the fall months. It's just as delicious.

Heat the olive oil in a large pot or Dutch oven over medium-low heat. Add the carrot, celery, and onion and sauté until the vegetables begin to soften, 8 to 10 minutes. Stir in the garlic, Italian seasoning, and chile flakes and sauté until fragrant, about 1 minute.

Stir in the vegetable broth, diced tomatoes, crushed tomatoes, and garlic powder. Season with salt and pepper. Cover the pot and simmer over medium heat until the carrots are tender, 10 to 15 minutes.

Uncover the pot and add the cheese tortellini. Cook until the pasta is just al dente, about 3 minutes. (The cook time may vary depending on the brand of tortellini.) Be careful to not overcook them; you want them just al dente because they will continue to expand and cook in the warm broth.

Reduce the heat to low. Once the broth has settled and is barely bubbling, stir in the spinach and heavy cream. Simmer just until the heavy cream has warmed and the spinach has wilted, 2 to 3 minutes. Taste and add more salt and pepper, if needed. Remove the pot from the heat.

Ladle the soup into individual bowls and serve with parmesan, basil, and a warm baguette, if desired. (Keep in mind that the tortellini will continue to expand as the soup cools, so you may need to add a little more broth to second servings or leftovers.)

Veganize it

Use unsweetened nondairy creamer for the heavy cream. Use a dairy-free tortellini, such as Kite Hill, or a plain hearty pasta shape, such as campanelle or mafalda, instead of the cheese tortellini.

Creamy WILD RICE SOUP

Serves 4 to 6

This is one of those stick-to-your-ribs kind of soups. And its thick and creamy broth makes it oh so cozy. Exactly what this section is about. Because the wild rice takes time to cook, I prefer to prepare it separately and add it near the end of the cooking process. That yields the best results. And to get that pretty golden broth, I typically use my Liquid Gold Vegetable Broth (page 68) or the Vegetarian No-Chicken Broth made by Imagine.

Make Ahead **You have a choice here:** You can make the wild rice ahead of time and set it aside or refrigerate up to 4 to 5 days. Or you can start the wild rice, and when it is about 30 minutes away from being done, start the soup. In either case, here's how you cook the wild rice: Bring the wild rice and 5 cups (1.2 liters) salted water to a boil in a medium saucepan over medium heat. Boil until the rice cracks or splits open on the sides, 45 to 60 minutes. Drain the rice and return it to the saucepan. Cover and set aside.

To start the soup, melt the butter in a large pot or Dutch oven over medium heat. Add the carrots, celery, onion, and mushrooms and sauté until the vegetables begin to soften, 8 to 10 minutes. Add the garlic and poultry seasoning and sauté until fragrant, about 1 minute. Sprinkle in the flour and stir continuously until it is thoroughly incorporated with the vegetables and turns slightly golden, 1 to 2 minutes.

Stir in the vegetable broth, thyme sprigs, and garlic powder. Bring to a boil over medium-high heat. Season with salt and pepper. Cover the pot and simmer over medium-low heat, stirring occasionally, until the carrots are tender, 10 to 15 minutes.

Uncover the soup, reduce the heat to low, and compost or discard the thyme sprigs. Stir in the cooked wild rice, kale, and heavy cream and simmer until the kale has wilted and cooked through, about 5 minutes. Taste and add more salt and pepper, if needed. Remove the pot from the heat.

Ladle the soup into individual bowls and serve. (Keep in mind that the soup will thicken as it cools, so you may need to add a little more broth to second servings or leftovers.)

½ cup (85 g) wild rice, rinsed (about 1½ cups once cooked)

Fine sea salt

5 tablespoons (75 g) unsalted butter

3 medium carrots, peeled and thinly sliced

2 medium celery stalks, thinly sliced

1 medium yellow onion, finely diced

8 ounces (225 g) cremini mushrooms, thinly sliced

3 garlic cloves, minced

¼ teaspoon poultry seasoning

¼ cup (31 g) all-purpose flour

4 cups (950 ml) vegetable broth, store-bought or homemade (page 68)

3 fresh thyme sprigs

¼ teaspoon garlic powder

Freshly ground black pepper to taste

2 cups (130 g) packed stemmed and thinly sliced curly or lacinato kale

1 cup (240 ml) heavy cream

Freestyle it

Substitutions for wild rice: dumplings, egg noodles, gnocchi, pasta

Substitutions for kale: spinach, Swiss chard

Veganize it

Use a neutral oil or a nondairy butter and unsweetened nondairy creamer for the heavy cream.

Michelle's Tip

Here's how you can use any wild rice left in the package you bought: Cook the wild rice and at the same time bake an acorn squash (halved). Stuff it with a combination of the cooked rice and sauteed plant-based sausage, mushrooms, kale, and shallots. Sprinkle with mozzarella and parmesan cheese and place under the broiler until melted and golden. Garnish with fresh sage sautéed in a little browned butter.

About That Chowder Life

Smoky
COLLARD GREEN CHOWDER
with Buttermilk Corn Bread

Serves 4 to 6

Buttermilk Corn Bread (recipe follows)

2 tablespoons extra-virgin olive oil

1 medium yellow onion, finely diced

4 garlic cloves, minced

6 or 7 young collard green leaves, thick stems removed and leaves sliced into strips ½ inch (1.3 cm) wide (about 5 cups/275 g)

1½ teaspoons smoked paprika

1 teaspoon Old Bay seasoning

1 teaspoon garlic powder

6½ cups (1.5 liters) vegetable broth, store-bought or homemade (page 68)

2 medium Yukon Gold potatoes, roughly chopped (about 2½ cups/350 g)

Fine sea salt and freshly ground black pepper to taste

2 small ears of corn, husked and cut or broken into 1½-inch (4 cm) pieces

1 cup (240 ml) unsweetened coconut milk

Hot sauce (optional), for serving

This rustic chowder is a result of wanting to work more hearty greens into my soups and stews. And I admit that I was a little on the fence as to whether or not I should call this a chowder. Loaded with potatoes and corn, with its smoky coconut broth—or should I say creamy "pot liquor"—I felt it was hearty enough to live up to its title. For this I buy a small bundle or handful of collard greens that I find in the organic produce section of the grocery store or a local farmers' market, as opposed to the larger 3-pound (1.4 kg) bunches. As for the corn, I prefer to leave it on the cob, but if you want to take the more traditional route, use 1 cup (145 g) corn kernels instead. The buttermilk corn bread is not a must, but it really goes well with all that creamy pot liquor goodness.

Make Ahead Make the corn bread as directed in the recipe and set aside until serving.

Make the chowder: Heat the olive oil in a large pot or Dutch oven over medium-low heat. Add the onion and sauté until softened, about 5 minutes. Throw in the garlic and sauté until fragrant, about 1 minute. Add the collard greens, smoked paprika, Old Bay, and garlic powder and stir until the spices are incorporated with the collard greens, about 1 minute.

Stir in the vegetable broth and potatoes. Season with salt and pepper. Cover the pot and simmer over medium heat until the potatoes are just fork-tender, 15 to 20 minutes.

Nestle the corn into the pot, cover, and cook until the corn is tender, 8 to 10 minutes. Uncover, reduce the heat to low, and stir in the coconut milk. Simmer for 3 to 5 minutes to let the flavors meld. Give it a taste and add more salt, if needed. Remove the pot from the heat.

Ladle the chowder into individual bowls and serve with a slice of that good ol' corn bread. Hit it with a few dashes of hot sauce, if desired.

Freestyle it

Substitutions for collard greens: kale, mustard greens, Swiss chard

Substitutions for potatoes: rutabaga, turnip

RECIPE CONTINUES ➞

BUTTERMILK CORN BREAD

Makes 8 slices

This is a savory corn bread . . . sorry sweet corn bread fans. In addition to serving with my Smoky Collard Green Chowder (page 120), it's also great as an accompaniment for other dishes such as my Smokin' Braised Collard Greens (page 193) and A Big Ol' Pot of Beans (page 208). And to switch things up a bit, you can add a little cheddar cheese, jalapeños, or even some sautéed corn or bell peppers to the corn bread batter, if you're feeling fancy.

1 cup (180 g) yellow or white cornmeal
1 cup (125 g) all-purpose flour
1 tablespoon baking powder
1½ teaspoons salt
1¼ cups (300 ml) buttermilk
1 large egg
5½ tablespoons (80 ml) canola oil
½ tablespoon (7 g) unsalted butter (optional)

Arrange an oven rack in the top one-third of the oven and preheat the oven to 425°F (220°C).

Whisk the cornmeal, all-purpose flour, baking powder, and salt in a large bowl. Whisk the buttermilk, egg, and 4 tablespoons (60 ml) of the canola oil in a small bowl. Add the buttermilk mixture to the cornmeal mixture and whisk thoroughly.

Once the oven is preheated, add the remaining 1½ tablespoons canola oil to a 9-inch (23 cm) pie pan or cast-iron skillet and place it in the oven for 2 to 3 minutes (this helps to create crispy edges).

Carefully remove the pan from the oven and use a flexible spatula to scrape the cornmeal batter evenly into the hot pan. Transfer the pan to the oven and bake until the top is golden, the edges are slightly browned, 20 to 25 minutes.

Remove the corn bread from the oven and, if using the butter, immediately top the corn bread with it. As it starts to melt, take a table knife and gently smear the butter over the top of the corn bread. Set it to the side to cool slightly. To store the corn bread, let it cool to room temperature and then wrap it tightly or store in an airtight container in the refrigerator for 5 to 7 days.

Vegetable-Cheddar
CHOWDER

Serves 4 to 6

This chowder is a family favorite and is widely loved by everyone who has tried it. Reason being . . . it's a little creamy . . . a little cheesy . . . and it's outrageously *good*! I enjoy making this any time of year, and it's a perfect way to use some of those frozen veggies that have been hanging out in my freezer for a while. If you like softer cauliflower and broccoli, cook them as directed below, but if you prefer them crisper, don't add them to the pot until the potatoes are almost soft. Additionally, if you'd like this soup to be a tad bit creamier, use an immersion blender to blend it several times just before stirring in the heavy cream and cheese.

Heat the olive oil in a large pot or Dutch oven over medium-low heat. Add the carrots, onion, and potato and sauté until the vegetables begin to soften, 8 to 10 minutes.

Add the garlic and sauté until fragrant, about 1 minute. Add the butter and once melted, sprinkle in the flour and stir continuously until it is thoroughly incorporated with the vegetables and turns slightly golden, 1 to 2 minutes. Stir in the vegetable broth, cauliflower, broccoli, corn, garlic powder, and bay leaf. Season lightly with salt and pepper. Cover the pot and simmer over medium-low heat, stirring occasionally, until the carrots and potatoes are fork-tender, 15 to 20 minutes.

Uncover and stir in the cream and cheddar. Reduce the heat to low and simmer until the cream has warmed and the cheese has melted, 2 to 3 minutes. Give it a taste and add more salt and pepper, if needed. Remove from the heat (compost or discard the bay leaf).

Ladle the chowder into bowls and serve with your favorite crackers.

3 tablespoons extra-virgin olive oil

2 medium carrots, peeled and thinly sliced

1 medium yellow onion, roughly chopped

1 large russet potato, peeled and roughly chopped (about 2 cups/ 280 g)

2 garlic cloves, minced

4 tablespoons (60 g) unsalted butter

¼ cup (31 g) all-purpose flour

4 cups (950 ml) vegetable broth, store-bought or homemade (page 68)

2 cups (270 g) cauliflower florets, fresh or frozen

2 cups (180 g) broccoli florets, fresh or frozen

1 cup (150 g) corn kernels, fresh, frozen, or canned

½ teaspoon garlic powder

1 bay leaf

Fine sea salt and freshly ground black pepper to taste

1 cup (240 ml) heavy cream (or half-and-half for a slightly lighter version)

5 ounces (140 g) coarsely grated sharp cheddar cheese (about 2 cups)

Crackers, for serving

Veganize it

Use a neutral oil or a nondairy butter in place of the dairy butter. Use unsweetened nondairy creamer for the heavy cream and meltable vegan cheese shreds or nutritional yeast for the cheddar.

SHRIMP & CORN
Chowder

Serves 4 to 6

4 tablespoons (60 g) unsalted butter

1 small yellow onion, finely diced

1 medium poblano pepper, seeded and finely diced (about ½ cup/75 g)

3 garlic cloves, minced

1 teaspoon dried oregano

3 tablespoons all-purpose flour

4 cups (950 ml) seafood broth or vegetable broth, store-bought or homemade (page 68)

Kernels from 2 ears fresh yellow corn (about 2 cups/290 g)

1 small zucchini, roughly chopped

1 teaspoon Old Bay seasoning

1 bay leaf

Fine sea salt and freshly ground black pepper to taste

1 pound (450 g) large shrimp, peeled and deveined, half roughly chopped

1 cup (240 ml) heavy cream (or half-and-half for a slightly lighter version)

Crackers (optional), for serving

This is one of my favorite chowders to make in the warmer months, when corn and zucchini are in abundance and taste so sweet and fresh. Unlike a lot of other chowders, this is a lighter one that does not involve potatoes—it's all about the shrimp, corn, and zucchini. For a little texture, I like to roughly chop half the shrimp and then leave the rest whole. That way you get a small piece of shrimp in almost every bite.

Melt the butter in a large pot or Dutch oven over medium-low heat. Add the onion and poblano pepper and sauté, stirring frequently, until the vegetables begin to soften, 5 to 7 minutes.

Add the garlic and oregano and sauté until fragrant, about 1 minute. Sprinkle in the flour and stir continuously until the flour is thoroughly incorporated with the vegetables and turns slightly golden, 1 to 2 minutes. Stir in the broth, corn, zucchini, Old Bay, and bay leaf. Season with salt and pepper. Cover the pot and simmer just until the zucchini begins to soften, 8 to 10 minutes.

Uncover, reduce the heat to low, and stir in the shrimp and heavy cream. Simmer until the shrimp are opaque and fully cooked, about 5 minutes. Give it a taste and add more salt and pepper, if needed. Remove the pot from the heat (compost or discard the bay leaf).

Ladle the chowder into individual bowls and serve with your favorite crackers (if using).

Veganize it

Use a neutral oil or a nondairy butter in place of the dairy butter. Use vegetable broth and unsweetened nondairy creamer for the heavy cream. Omit the shrimp and consider adding in some cauliflower when you add in the corn and zucchini.

$Smoky$ SALMON CHOWDER

Serves 4 to 6

SALMON

1 (12-ounce/340 g) skin-on salmon fillet

Extra-virgin olive oil, for drizzling

½ teaspoon smoked paprika

Fine sea salt and freshly ground black pepper to taste

CHOWDER

4 tablespoons (60 g) unsalted butter

2 medium Yukon Gold potatoes, roughly chopped (about 2 cups/280 g)

1 small yellow onion, finely diced

1 medium celery stalk, thinly sliced

2 garlic cloves, minced

3 tablespoons all-purpose flour

4 cups (950 ml) seafood broth or vegetable broth, store-bought or homemade (page 68)

Kernels from 1 ear fresh yellow corn (about 1 cup/145 g)

2 tablespoons tomato paste

1 tablespoon nonpareil capers, drained

¼ teaspoon smoked paprika

1 bay leaf

Worcestershire sauce

Fine sea salt and freshly ground black pepper to taste

1 heaping tablespoon cream cheese

¾ cup (175 ml) heavy cream

FOR SERVING

Chopped fresh dill leaves (optional)

Oyster crackers or saltines

Several years ago, Alex and I traveled to Seattle and I was so excited because I was finally able to check off one of the restaurants that had been on my bucket list for years: Pike Place Chowder. We stood in line for what seemed an eternity and I ordered the chowder sampler, so that I could taste several of their chowders, including the smoked salmon chowder. After we got home, I was still craving it and this chowder is a result of those cravings. I've posted this several times on Instagram and so many of you have asked for the recipe. Well, this is for you. I prefer to season the salmon lightly with smoked paprika and then bake it because it's so moist that way. However, I've also used leftover grilled salmon and smoked trout, which work great, too. And if you don't want to be bothered with all of that and prefer to purchase salmon that has already been smoked, then there's that option as well.

Prepare the salmon: Arrange an oven rack in the top one-third of the oven and preheat the oven to 425°F (220°C). Line a sheet pan with foil or parchment paper.

Set the salmon on a plate skin side down. Pat dry, drizzle with a little olive oil, and sprinkle with the smoked paprika. Season with salt and pepper. Transfer the salmon to the lined pan skin side down. Bake until slightly golden on top and opaque in the center, 10 to 18 minutes (depending on thickness). Once done, cover with foil and set aside.

Make the chowder: Melt the butter in a large pot or Dutch oven over medium-low heat. Once melted, add the potatoes, onion, and celery and sauté, stirring often, until the vegetables begin to soften, 8 to 10 minutes.

Add the garlic and sauté until fragrant, about 1 minute. Sprinkle the flour into the pot and stir continuously until the flour is thoroughly incorporated with the vegetables and it turns slightly golden, 1 to 2 minutes. Stir in the broth, corn, tomato paste, capers, smoked paprika, bay leaf, and a few dashes Worcestershire sauce. Season with salt and pepper. Cover the pot and simmer over medium-low heat, stirring occasionally, until the potatoes are fork-tender, 15 to 20 minutes.

Uncover, reduce the heat to low, add the cream cheese, and stir until the cream cheese is melted. Stir in the heavy cream.

Use a fork to flake the salmon into large chunks (compost or discard the skin). Add the flaked salmon to the pot, gently stir to incorporate the salmon into the chowder, and simmer for 5 more minutes to let the flavors meld. Give it a taste and add more salt and pepper, if needed. Remove the pot from the heat (compost or discard the bay leaf).

Ladle the chowder into individual bowls, garnish with fresh dill (if using) and serve with oyster crackers.

White Fish & LEEK CHOWDER

Serves 4 to 6

I don't have many stories to share about my father because he was not a part of my life for very long—but I remember he *loved* to get up early every weekend morning to go fishing. I know you may be asking, what does that have to do with this delicious chowder . . . well nothing, really, other than the fact that my love for seafood was probably instilled by him early on. After a long day of fishing, he would come home and fry up his catches from the day and serve them with a big pot of spaghetti and a few slices of white bread—a tradition passed down by my grandmother. This is a rustic brothy chowder and I like to use a firm yet tender fish that holds up well, such as haddock, halibut, cod, or grouper. If you like a little spice in your life, I highly recommend adding a few dashes of hot sauce when serving. It's just something about that little hit of spicy-vinegary twang that makes me do a happy dance in the kitchen.

Melt the butter in a large pot or Dutch oven over medium-low heat. Add the leeks and sauté until softened, 8 to 10 minutes, stirring frequently.

Add the garlic and smoked paprika and sauté until fragrant, about 1 minute. Pour in the vermouth and scrape the bottom of the pan to deglaze it. Sauté until the alcohol has cooked off, 1 to 2 minutes. Stir in the seafood broth, clam juice, potatoes, thyme sprigs, bay leaf, and Worcestershire sauce. Season with salt and pepper. Cover the pot and simmer over medium heat, stirring occasionally, until the potatoes are fork-tender, 15 to 20 minutes.

Uncover, reduce the heat to low, and stir in the corn and heavy cream. Carefully nestle the fish fillets into the broth and season lightly with salt and pepper. Cover the pot and simmer undisturbed until the fish flakes easily with a fork and is cooked through, 8 to 10 minutes.

Give the chowder a gentle stir, breaking the fish into nice-size chunks. Remove the pot from the heat (compost or discard the bay leaf and thyme sprigs). Give it a taste and add more salt and pepper, if needed.

Ladle the chowder into individual bowls and top each with some grinds of black pepper. If desired, serve with your favorite hot sauce (Yassss!) and some oyster crackers.

Veganize it

Use cauliflower instead of fish, vegan wine or vegetable broth for deglazing, substitute vegetable broth for the clam juice, and use a neutral oil or nondairy butter, vegan Worcestershire sauce, and unsweetened nondairy creamer for the heavy cream.

3 tablespoons (45 g) unsalted butter

2 thin leeks, white and light-green parts only, halved lengthwise, fanned out, thoroughly rinsed, and thinly sliced crosswise

3 garlic cloves, minced

½ teaspoon smoked paprika

¼ cup (60 ml) dry vermouth or dry white wine

4 cups (950 ml) seafood broth or vegetable broth, store-bought or homemade (page 68)

1 cup (8 ounces/240 ml) clam juice

1 pound (450 g) petite Yukon Gold potatoes, halved

3 fresh thyme sprigs

1 bay leaf

½ teaspoon Worcestershire sauce

Fine sea salt and freshly ground black pepper to taste

1 cup (150 g) corn kernels, fresh, frozen, or canned

1 cup (240 ml) heavy cream

2 haddock, cod, halibut, or grouper fillets (8 ounces/225 g each)

FOR SERVING

Freshly ground black pepper

Hot sauce (optional), such as Texas Pete or Frank's RedHot or your favorite kind

Oyster crackers or saltines (optional)

Let's Top It!

Whether it's dollops, drizzles, or an array of crunchy bits, toppings are what add that extra flare to a soup. Any of the soups in this chapter can be dressed up or down, however you see fit. Here are a few topping ideas and recipes that will help take your soups (or salads) to the next level:

Crispy and Crunchy Bits: baked cereal, chips, crackers, crispy beans or lentils, crostini, croutons, fried capers, fried garlic, fried shallots/onions, grilled cheese croutons, parmesan crisps, raw vegetables, savory granola, seeds, toasted coconut, toasted quinoa, toasted nuts

Dollops: crushed Calabrian peppers, mascarpone, pesto, pistou, plain yogurt, ricotta, sour cream

Drizzles and Swirls: citrus juice (lemons/limes), coconut milk, fish sauce, hot chili oil, chili crisp, hot sauce, infused oils, olive oil, toasted sesame oil, truffle oil, tamari, vinegar

Other Embellishments: cinnamon, citrus zest, fresh herbs, fried herbs, grains, grated/shredded/crumbled cheese, nutmeg, pasta, sumac

Crispy Wonton Strips

Makes 2 cups (45 g)

Canola oil
10 (3¼-inch/8 cm) square wonton wrappers (see Michelle's Tip), such as Nasoya, cut into ½-inch (1.3 cm) strips
Fine sea salt

Line a plate with paper towels and have at the ready. Pour 1 inch (2.5 cm) canola oil into a medium skillet and set over medium heat until hot. (You can test by adding 1 wonton strip to the oil to see if it sizzles as soon as it hits the oil.)

Working in small batches, add the strips to the oil and fry just until golden, about 1 minute. Use a slotted spoon to transfer the strips to the paper towels to drain. Lightly season the cooked strips with salt and set aside until you're ready to use them. Store any leftovers in an airtight container at room temperature for up to 4 days.

Michelle's Tip

Store the unused wrappers in a freezer-safe container and freeze for up to 1 year.

Halloumi Croutons

Makes about 2 cups (275 g)

8 ounces (225 g) Halloumi cheese, cut into slices ¼ inch (6 mm) thick
2 tablespoons canola oil
2 teaspoons pure maple syrup
2 tablespoons unsalted roasted pumpkin seeds

Pat the Halloumi slices dry with a paper towel and tear them into bite-size pieces.

Heat the canola oil in a large nonstick skillet over medium heat. Add the Halloumi pieces to the skillet and fry until both sides are golden in color, 3 to 5 minutes, flipping once. Remove the skillet from the heat and stir in the maple syrup and pumpkin seeds. Let them cool slightly and then serve immediately. (If you're not planning on serving an entire pot of soup at one time, you may want to halve this recipe.)

Herby Croutons

Makes about 4 cups (230 g)

6 ounces (170 g) artisanal bread, torn into bite-size
   pieces (about 4 cups)
¼ cup (60 ml) extra-virgin olive oil
1 teaspoon Italian seasoning
½ teaspoon garlic powder
¼ teaspoon fine sea salt, or to taste

Arrange an oven rack in the top one-third of the oven and
preheat the oven to 375°F (190°C).

Toss the bread, olive oil, Italian seasoning, garlic powder,
and salt in a large bowl. Spread the croutons out evenly
on a sheet pan. Transfer the pan to the oven and bake
until the croutons are golden and crispy, 15 to 20 minutes,
tossing halfway through.

Set aside to cool. Store in an airtight container at room
temperature until ready to use or for up to 4 days.

Pico de Gallo

Makes about 2 cups (345 g)

3 medium Roma or vine-ripened tomatoes, halved,
   seeded, and finely diced
¼ cup (30 g) finely diced sweet onion
¼ cup (7 g) loosely packed fresh cilantro leaves,
   roughly chopped
1 small jalapeño, seeded and finely diced
Juice of 1 small lime
Fine sea salt to taste

Combine the tomatoes, onion, cilantro, jalapeño, lime
juice, and salt in a small bowl. Store in the refrigerator in
an airtight container until you're ready to use or for up to
2 days.

Spiced Tortilla Strips

Makes about 3 cups (115 g)

Canola oil
5 (5½- to 6-inch/14 to 15 cm) white or yellow corn
   tortillas, cut into ½-inch (1.3 cm) strips
Chili powder
Fine sea salt

Line a plate with paper towels and have at the ready. Pour
enough canola oil into a medium skillet to come halfway up
the sides and set over medium heat and heat until hot. (You
can test by adding 1 tortilla strip to the oil to see if it sizzles
as soon as it hits the oil.)

Working in batches, add a handful of strips at a time to the
oil and fry just until golden, 1 to 3 minutes. Use a slotted
spoon to transfer the strips to the paper towels to drain.
Lightly season the strips with salt and chili powder and set
aside until ready to use. Store any leftovers in an airtight
container at room temperature for up to 4 days.

Herby Croutons,
page 133

Spiced
Tortilla Strips,
page 133

Pico de Gallo,
page 133

Crispy Wonton
Strips, page 132

Halloumi
Croutons,
page 132

Handy
THINGS

Had I had more pages, this chapter surely would have been longer, because pizza, sandwiches, wraps, tacos, and quesadillas—basically all of the "handy" (handheld) foods—are some of my go-to meals, especially during the week. Are all of those in this chapter? No . . . but a few of my favorites are.

The Panzanella-ish
PIZZA

Serves 4

12 ounces (340 g) tomatoes, diced and/or sliced

½ cup (15 g) loosely packed fresh basil leaves, roughly chopped, plus more for topping

⅓ cup (40 g) thinly sliced red onion

1 garlic clove, finely grated

1 tablespoon nonpareil capers

1 tablespoon extra-virgin olive oil, plus more for drizzling

2 teaspoons red wine vinegar

Fine sea salt and freshly ground black pepper to taste

1 pound (450 g) pizza dough, store-bought or homemade

All-purpose flour for dusting

3 ounces (85 g) spreadable soft cheese, such as Boursin Garlic & Fine Herbs

Freestyle it

Substitutions for Boursin cheese: burrata, herby goat cheese, ricotta, stracciatella, whipped feta

Other ideas to consider: Add a drizzle of Balsamic Glaze (page 64) on top; instead of the salad, use roasted broccoli rabe topped with lemon zest and parmesan; roasted fall squash with brown butter fried sage; grilled zucchini/squash, corn, and fresh basil.

Veganize it

Use dairy-free Boursin Garlic & Herb cheese or something comparable.

This fabulous pizza is a riff on the classic panzanella salad, but the only "bread" involved is the pizza base. Just imagine that crispy crust with the ripest summer salad on top. It's so good! When picking tomatoes for this recipe, I find it fun to use a mixture of different types of heirloom tomatoes of various colors and sizes. If heirlooms are not available, use a different variety. As for the cheese, I like to experiment and use soft spreadable types of herby cheese such as Boursin, but goat cheese, fresh mozzarella, or even burrata are nice as well. Many store-bought pizza doughs need to sit at room temperature for at least 30 minutes and up to 3 hours to rise, so keep that in mind when preparing your dough. It will make it a little easier to stretch and flatten out the dough. And for faster cleanup, cover the counter with several pieces of beeswax wrap and then dust that with flour. When it's time to clean up, carefully pull all sides of the wrap up, compost or discard the flour, and clean the beeswax wrap.

Make the salad: Combine the tomatoes, basil, red onion, garlic, capers, olive oil, and vinegar in a large bowl. Lightly toss together, taste, and season with salt and pepper. Set aside to let the flavors marry, at least 15 minutes. Drain any juice that collects at the bottom of the bowl.

Arrange an oven rack in the top one-third of the oven and preheat the oven to 450°F (230°C). Line a sheet pan with parchment paper.

Make the pizza: Place the dough on a lightly floured surface. Using your fingers, gently press and stretch the dough out to form a round or rectangular shape (at least 12 inches/30 cm in diameter or length). If the dough is too sticky, lightly dust it with some flour. Transfer the dough to the lined pan. Gently press it out more, if needed. Drizzle the dough lightly with olive oil.

Transfer the sheet pan to the oven and bake until golden and crispy, 10 to 12 minutes.

Remove from the oven, let the crust cool slightly, then smear a thin layer of the spreadable cheese evenly on top of the crust. Spoon the salad on top and drizzle with a little olive oil. (Goodness that looks good!)

Use a pizza cutter or sharp knife to cut the crust into equal slices, top with fresh basil, and serve immediately.

Banging
TOFU LETTUCE WRAPS

Serves 2 (with leftovers)

Many years ago, I worked part-time at a P.F. Chang's restaurant. One of the dishes that I usually ordered before my shift was tofu lettuce wraps. Yeah . . . I'll admit that I was kind of hooked on them. And although my time working there was short, my love for them continues with these banging (aka delicious) tofu lettuce wraps. What I like most about this tofu mixture is that it is also terrific over rice, in stir-fries, and in dumplings, as well as tossed with noodles.

Make the sauce: Whisk together the tamari, sesame oil, honey, Sriracha sauce, vinegar, garlic, and ginger in a small bowl and set aside.

Prepare the tofu and wraps: Heat the canola oil in a large nonstick or cast-iron skillet over medium-high heat. Crumble the tofu into the skillet and cook, stirring occasionally and breaking up any large pieces with the tip of a silicone spatula, until the tofu starts to look golden and slightly crispy, similar to scrambled eggs, 11 to 13 minutes.

Add the scallions, carrot, and water chestnuts and continue to brown the tofu for 1 to 2 minutes. Pour the sauce over the tofu mixture and stir. Reduce the heat to medium and cook, stirring occasionally, until most of the liquid has cooked off the tofu, about 5 minutes. Remove the skillet from the heat.

If using Bibb lettuce, peel off the desired number of leaves to be used as the cups to hold the tofu mixture; if using iceberg lettuce, gently peel off some of the lettuce layers. Transfer to a platter. Spoon the tofu mixture into the lettuce cups. If desired, serve with scallions, tamari, and Sriracha sauce.

SAUCE

3 tablespoons tamari or soy sauce

1 tablespoon toasted sesame oil

1 tablespoon honey

1 teaspoon Sriracha sauce

1 teaspoon unseasoned rice vinegar

1 garlic clove, finely grated

1 teaspoon grated fresh ginger

TOFU AND WRAPS

3 tablespoons canola oil

1 (14-ounce/397 g) package extra-firm tofu, drained and pressed (see How to Press Tofu, page 18)

2 scallions, thinly sliced (optional), plus more for serving

1 medium carrot, peeled and coarsely shredded (about ½ cup/55 g)

1 (8-ounce/225 g) can sliced water chestnuts, drained and roughly chopped

1 small head Bibb lettuce, or ½ head iceberg lettuce

Tamari and Sriracha sauce (optional), for serving

Veganize it

Use pure maple syrup, agave nectar, brown sugar, or another sweetener of your choice instead of honey.

Cheesy Mushroom
FRENCH DIP

Serves 2 to 4

FILLING

2 tablespoons canola oil

12 ounces (340 g) cremini or portobello mushrooms (or more, depending on length of the baguette), thinly sliced

1 small red or green bell pepper, thinly sliced

1 teaspoon Worcestershire sauce

½ teaspoon smoked paprika

½ teaspoon Italian seasoning

Fine sea salt and freshly ground black pepper to taste

AU JUS

1 tablespoon (15 g) unsalted butter

½ small yellow onion, finely diced

¼ teaspoon smoked paprika

¼ teaspoon ground black pepper

1½ cups (360 ml) vegetable broth, store-bought or homemade (page 68)

1 tablespoon tamari or soy sauce

1 teaspoon Worcestershire sauce

Fine sea salt to taste

SANDWICHES

1 baguette or artisanal loaf (12 to 16 inches/30 to 40 cm long) as wide as you can find

4 to 6 slices smoked provolone cheese

When I stopped eating beef, there were two sandwiches that I missed: French dips with au jus and Philly cheesesteaks. This is a representation of my love for both in hearty sandwich form, but I use a flavorful combination of mushrooms and bell peppers instead. And let's not forget that au jus, so that you can dip, baby, dip!

Make the filling: Heat the canola oil in a large nonstick or cast-iron skillet over medium-high heat. Add the mushrooms, spreading them out as evenly as possible in the skillet. Cook, undisturbed, for about 5 minutes and then give them a stir. Stir in the bell pepper, Worcestershire sauce, smoked paprika, and Italian seasoning. Season lightly with salt and pepper. Sauté until the mushrooms are browned and most of the moisture has cooked off, 3 to 5 minutes. Give it a taste and add more salt and pepper, if needed. Transfer the mixture to a medium bowl and set aside.

Make the au jus: Use the same skillet (no need to clean it) to melt the butter over medium-low heat. Add the onion and sauté until softened, 3 to 5 minutes. Add the smoked paprika and black pepper and sauté until fragrant, about 30 seconds. Stir in the vegetable broth, tamari, and Worcestershire sauce. Bring the broth to a boil over medium heat, then reduce the heat to low and simmer for 5 minutes to let the flavors meld and onion soften a bit more. Give it a taste and add salt or more tamari, if needed. Remove the skillet from the heat.

Prepare the sandwiches: Preheat the oven to 400°F (200°C).

Halve the baguette lengthwise. Open the baguette and place it, cut side up, on a large sheet pan. Transfer to the oven and lightly toast, 4 to 5 minutes. Remove from the oven and preheat the broiler to high. Divide the mushroom mixture between the baguette halves. Layer the cheese slices over the mushroom mixture.

Place the sheet pan under the broiler to melt the cheese and reheat the mushroom mixture, 1 to 2 minutes. Be sure to watch it carefully so that the sandwich does not burn. Remove from the broiler and fold the halves together.

Cut into 4 pieces, plate, and ladle the au jus into small bowls to serve alongside for dipping. This baby gets juicy, so don't forget to grab some extra napkins for everyone.

Veganize it

Use nondairy butter, vegan Worcestershire sauce, and omit the cheese or use vegan cheese slices.

Avocado-Pesto SUBS

Serves 2

The simplicity of this sub is right up there with tomato and mayonnaise or pimento cheese sandwiches. I love the combination of avocados, tomatoes, fresh mozzarella, and the basil pesto that makes this sub sing! If you have any baby spinach or arugula on hand, you can use some of that as well: Use 1 cup (30 g) of basil and 1 cup (20 g) of baby spinach or arugula. And if you don't have time to make pesto, store-bought works fine. Use any leftover pesto on a grilled cheese sandwich, pizza, or stir it into some plain rice or brothy butter beans topped with a poached egg or another protein for a satisfying and quick dinner.

Make Ahead
Make the pesto as directed and refrigerate until serving. Preheat the broiler to high heat.

Open the ciabatta and place on a large sheet pan, cut side up. Drizzle with olive oil and place under the broiler for 1 to 2 minutes, just to toast and warm the bread. (Be sure to watch it so that it does not burn.) Transfer to a serving plate.

Smear several tablespoons of pesto onto one or both sides of the loaf. Generously layer with the mozzarella, tomatoes, and avocado. Close the sub, halve it, and serve immediately.

BASIL PESTO

Makes about ¾ cup (165 g)

2 cups (60 g) loosely packed fresh basil leaves
2 tablespoons pine nuts
2 tablespoons freshly grated parmesan cheese
1 tablespoon fresh lemon juice
1 garlic clove, peeled but whole
⅛ teaspoon fine sea salt, or to taste
⅛ teaspoon ground black pepper
¼ cup (60 ml) extra-virgin olive oil

Combine the basil, pine nuts, parmesan, lemon juice, garlic, salt, and black pepper in a small food processor. Pulse several times. With the machine running, slowly drizzle in the olive oil. Use a silicone spatula to scrape down the sides of the bowl and continue blending, until almost smooth. Give it a taste and add more salt and pepper, if needed. Transfer the pesto to a small airtight container and refrigerate until ready to serve or for up to 4 to 5 days.

¼ cup Basil Pesto, or more if desired (recipe follows)

1 (12-inch/30 cm) ciabatta loaf or baguette, halved lengthwise

Extra-virgin olive oil, for drizzling

4 to 6 ounces (115 to 170 g) fresh mozzarella cheese, thinly sliced

1 large vine-ripened tomato, thinly sliced

1 large avocado, thinly sliced

Freestyle it

Substitutions for avocado: sautéed broccoli rabe, roasted asparagus, roasted eggplant

Substitutions for pine nuts in the Basil Pesto: almonds, pecans, walnuts

Other additions to consider: a drizzle of Balsamic Glaze (page 64), spicy mayonnaise

Veganize it

Omit the mozzarella cheese or use vegan mozzarella cheese in the sandwich. For the Basil Pesto: Omit the parmesan cheese and use 1 tablespoon of nutritional yeast and 1 teaspoon of white miso paste instead.

Michelle's Tip

To make a pistou (which I like to use as a topping on various soups), simply omit the nuts in this recipe.

My Favorite
HUMMUS & KALE WRAP

Serves 4

4 to 8 tablespoons My Favorite Hummus (recipe follows)

KALE FILLING

6 cups (390 g) packed stemmed and roughly chopped curly or lacinato kale

2 tablespoons extra-virgin olive oil

2 tablespoons nutritional yeast, or more to taste

1 tablespoon mayonnaise

½ teaspoon smoked paprika

½ teaspoon garlic powder

Drizzle of red wine vinegar

Kernels from 1 ear fresh yellow corn (½ cup/75 g cooked corn, if making off-season)

½ cup (90 g) diced tomatoes

1 small avocado, diced

Fine sea salt and freshly ground black pepper to taste

FOR ASSEMBLY

4 (10-inch/25 cm) spinach or sun-dried tomato wraps

Chips, for serving (optional)

My love for kale came later in life when my friend Jamila made me one of her well-known kale salads. She added nutritional yeast (also known as "nooch"), an ingredient that was new to me at the time. It made the salad slightly creamy and cheesy tasting without the addition of cheese. After her introduction, I began incorporating more kale and nutritional yeast into my meals, and this wrap is one of many ways I like to do that. For the filling, I add a lot of fresh ingredients, which can easily be swapped depending on the season. Consider the following recipe for my favorite hummus as a starting point and you can add other things (roasted garlic, roasted red bell peppers, harissa, etc.) to flavor it in the future. And if you don't have time to make hummus, no worries; store-bought works well too.

Make Ahead Make the hummus as directed in the recipe and refrigerate until ready to use.

Make the kale filling: Place the kale in a large bowl. Drizzle the olive oil over the kale and massage with your hands until the kale is thoroughly coated and a slightly darker shade of green. Add the nutritional yeast, mayonnaise, smoked paprika, garlic powder, and vinegar and toss together to incorporate. Lightly toss in the corn, tomatoes, and avocado. Season with salt and pepper.

Assemble the wraps: Smear 1 to 2 tablespoons of hummus onto the center of each wrap. Place one-quarter of the salad filling on the bottom portion of each wrap. Fold two sides to the center, then fold the bottom toward the center and continue to roll. Pin with a toothpick or wrap with parchment paper to hold it together, if needed. Serve with your favorite chips, if desired.

Freestyle it

Substitutions for nutritional yeast: 1 to 2 tablespoons feta cheese or freshly grated parmesan cheese

Veganize it

Use vegan mayonnaise.

MY FAVORITE HUMMUS

Makes about 1½ cups (360 g)

1 (15-ounce/425 g) can chickpeas, liquid drained into a small bowl and reserved

½ teaspoon baking soda

½ teaspoon fine sea salt, or to taste

3 tablespoons well-stirred tahini

Juice of ½ medium lemon, or more to taste

1 small garlic clove, smashed

¼ teaspoon ground cumin

1 tablespoon extra-virgin olive oil, plus more for drizzling

Combine the chickpeas, baking soda, salt, and 4 cups (950 ml) water in a medium saucepan and bring to a rapid simmer over medium-low heat. Boil just until you start to see the outer skins separate from the chickpeas, 15 to 20 minutes. Drain (no need to remove the skins).

Transfer the chickpeas, tahini, lemon juice, 3 to 4 tablespoons of the reserved chickpea liquid, garlic, cumin, and olive oil to a food processor. Blend until very smooth, about 1 minute. Use a silicone spatula to scrape down the sides of the bowl and continue blending, if needed. If the consistency is too thick, with the machine running, add more chickpea liquid or cold water 1 tablespoon at a time, until it's the desired consistency. Give it a taste and add more lemon juice or salt, if needed.

Transfer the hummus to an airtight container and store in the refrigerator for up to 3 to 4 days.

TUNA & EGG SALAD SAMMIES

Serves 2 (with leftovers)

There are many different ways to make tuna and egg salad, but this was Mom's favorite way to make it. It has become highly requested over the years, especially by my good friend Michelle (her name is Michelle too). So, Michelle, this is for the times that I can't be there to make it for you. (Smile.) If you're not in the mood for a sandwich, this salad goes well on top of leafy salads, and it's also fantastic with crackers or thick chips. I also use this mixture to make tuna and egg pasta salad (for that I typically use roughly 8 ounces/225 g of cooked pasta and add a few additional tablespoons of mayonnaise).

Make the tuna and egg salad: Combine the chopped boiled eggs, tuna, mayonnaise, and sweet pickle relish in a medium bowl. Season with salt and pepper and lightly mix together. Give it a taste and add more salt and pepper, if needed.

Make the sandwiches: Place 1 slice of bread on each of two serving plates. Layer on some of the tuna and egg salad, along with the lettuce, Havarti cheese, tomatoes and pickle slices, and shower on a few potato chips (if using). Top with the remaining slices of bread and serve. (Go on with your bad self!)

TUNA AND EGG SALAD

3 large Hard-Boiled Eggs (page 31), roughly chopped

2 (5-ounce/142 g) cans water-packed wild-caught chunk light tuna, drained

½ cup (112 g) mayonnaise (or a little less, if you prefer)

3 tablespoons sweet pickle relish

Fine sea salt and freshly ground black pepper to taste

SANDWICHES

4 slices artisanal bread

2 cups (110 g) thinly sliced iceberg lettuce

2 to 4 slices Havarti cheese or your favorite sliced cheese

1 large vine-ripened tomato, thinly sliced

4 to 6 dill pickle sandwich slices

Plain potato chips (optional)

Tuna SANDWICHES
with Sun-Dried Tomato Aioli

Serves 4

AIOLI AND TUNA MIXTURE

½ cup (112 g) mayonnaise

2 tablespoons minced drained oil-packed sun-dried tomatoes

1 small garlic clove, finely grated

2 (5-ounce/142 g) cans water-packed wild-caught chunk light tuna, drained

SPINACH SALAD

4 cups (80 g) loosely packed baby spinach or arugula, roughly chopped

½ cup (56 g) pitted Castelvetrano olives, roughly chopped

⅓ cup (40 g) thinly sliced red onion

A good drizzle of extra-virgin olive oil

A squeeze of fresh lemon juice or splash of red wine vinegar

Fine sea salt and freshly ground black pepper to taste

SANDWICHES

1 (10-inch/25 cm) focaccia bread or ciabatta loaf, split in half

6 slices provolone cheese (Muenster or Havarti are great, too)

1 large tomato, thinly sliced

½ medium English cucumber, thinly peeled into long strips or ribbons

I know you're thinking, more tuna? And the answer is yes. But for good reason, because the sun-dried tomato aioli in this sandwich is game-changing. After trying this sandwich, my friend Gudrun and her husband, Todd, suggested that it would be better if I mixed the aioli in with the tuna, so I did, and it's ridiculously good. This sandwich is fully loaded with all of those beautiful layers, so I recommend making it on a wider bread such as a focaccia or ciabatta loaf. It will give you a bigger playing field for all of the toppings and you won't have to worry about everything falling out.

Make the aioli and tuna mixture: Vigorously mix the mayonnaise, sun-dried tomatoes, and garlic in a small bowl. The sun-dried tomatoes should be fully incorporated (the aioli will be a light pink or salmon color).

Flake the tuna into a separate small bowl and add your desired amount of aioli (I usually add all of it). Mix thoroughly.

Make the spinach salad: Combine the spinach, olives, red onion, olive oil, and lemon juice in a medium bowl. Season with salt and pepper and lightly toss together.

Make the sandwiches: Smear the tuna mixture onto the bottom piece of bread and layer with the provolone, tomato, and cucumber. Pile on the spinach salad. Top with the other bread half, cut it into 4 sections, and serve with extra napkins. (Now that's a sandwich!)

Freestyle it

Other ideas to consider: One of my recipe testers suggested that this would be a great tuna melt situation, and I agree. To do that, layer the tuna onto the bread and top it with the cheese. Place it on a sheet pan under the broiler on high until the cheese has melted, 1 to 2 minutes. Then proceed to make the rest of the sandwich.

Veganize it

Omit the tuna and use 1 (15-ounce/425 g) can chickpeas that has been drained, rinsed, and then roughly smashed to retain some texture. Use vegan mayonnaise in the aioli (I usually use about ⅓ cup/75 ml of the mixture) and use vegan cheese slices.

Brinner?

Brinner was kind of a thing in our house growing up. We never called it that, but we often had what a lot of us consider breakfast for dinner. Breakfast was one of the first meals that I ventured to cook. It normally consisted of a big bowl of cheese grits, bacon or sausage, and sometimes a fried or scrambled egg. What I enjoy most about the recipes in this chapter is that they can be eaten any time of the day.

Savory
COTTAGE CHEESE FOR ONE

Serves 1

This is one of those easy meals that I usually prepare for myself because Alex is not a fan of cottage cheese. I, on the other hand, think cottage cheese is great because you can either dress it up with sweet accompaniments or you can take the savory route, which I've done here. As a child, Mom and I would go to our neighborhood Piccadilly Cafeteria *a lot*. And one of the things that she would always order, aside from the "Dilly Plate," was their cottage cheese and pear salad. Well, back then you couldn't have paid me to eat it, but I eventually grew to understand why she always ordered it. This combination is one that I particularly enjoy, but I encourage you to play around with the toppings based on what you like or have on hand.

¾ cup (158 g) cottage cheese

6 to 8 cherry or grape tomatoes, halved

½ small avocado, thinly sliced

1 large Hard-Boiled Egg (page 31), halved

Toasted sesame oil

Everything bagel seasoning

Minced scallions

Put the cottage cheese in a bowl, then add the cherry tomatoes, avocado, and hard-boiled egg. Top with a drizzle of sesame oil, a sprinkle of everything bagel seasoning, and a scattering of scallions.

For the Love of
HASH BROWNS CASSEROLE

Serves 6 to 8

20 ounces (570 g) shredded hash brown potatoes, store-bought (such as Simply Potatoes) or home-shredded

1½ tablespoons canola oil, plus more as needed

6 vegetarian sausage patties, such as MorningStar Farms

½ medium yellow onion, roughly chopped

1 medium red or green bell pepper, roughly chopped (or do half of each for a pop of color)

12 large eggs

1¼ cups (300 ml) whole milk

1 teaspoon Italian seasoning

½ teaspoon garlic powder

½ teaspoon fine sea salt, plus more to taste

¼ teaspoon ground black pepper, plus more to taste

Pinch of red chile flakes (optional)

12 ounces (340 g) sharp cheddar cheese, shredded (about 3 cups)

Ketchup (optional), for serving

I LOVE hash browns! No. Really, I do. And this fun casserole does not disappoint. I typically make this early on Sunday mornings before Alex wakes up, because it makes the house smell divine! I mean . . . who doesn't love to wake up to the smell of breakfast cooking?! This bad boy can feed a lot, so it's perfect for serving at larger family or friendly gatherings . . . or do like we do and eat the leftovers as quick meals during the week.

Before you get started: If using frozen shredded hash browns, thaw them in the baking dish for at least 15 to 30 minutes prior to adding the other ingredients. If using real potatoes, grate them on the large holes of a box grater. Put the potatoes in a fine-mesh sieve and rinse under cold water and drain well. Transfer the potatoes to a clean kitchen towel and wring out any excess water.

Preheat the oven to 350°F (180°C).

Heat the canola oil in a large nonstick skillet over medium-low heat. Add the sausage patties and cook on each side until they are slightly browned, 3 to 5 minutes. Transfer to a plate to cool, then give them a rough chop.

Use the same skillet (no need to clean it) and add the onion and bell pepper. Drizzle in a little more oil, if needed, and sauté until the vegetables begin to soften, 4 to 5 minutes.

Crack the eggs into a large bowl and add the milk, Italian seasoning, garlic powder, salt, black pepper, and chile flakes and whisk together. Put the hash browns in a 9 × 13-inch (23 x 33 cm) baking dish with the chopped sausage, onion/bell pepper mixture, and 1½ cups (170 g) of the cheddar and stir to combine. Season liberally with salt and pepper and give it one more stir.

Pour the egg mixture evenly over the top of the hash brown mixture. Sprinkle the rest of the cheddar on top, transfer to the oven, and bake until the top is golden and the cheese is melted, 40 to 45 minutes. Let the casserole rest for 5 minutes before serving. If desired, serve ketchup alongside.

Freestyle it

Substitutions for vegetarian sausage patties: Sauté 8 ounces (225 g) of mushrooms in a little oil. Season with smoked paprika and cook until golden and browned.

Other additions to consider: chives, kale, scallions, spinach

Cheesy GRITS

with Mushrooms, Tomatoes & Spinach

Serves 2

Grits have always been a staple in our house. And for this grits bowl, I take a different approach and load them with some of my favorite sautéed veggies and a good drizzle of smoked paprika butter, rather than the things you typically see like shrimp, fish, or sausage. One thing to note about grits: they can vary in texture and the cooking time can differ based on how fine the corn has been ground. Fine-ground grits take the least amount of time to cook. However, medium to coarse stone-ground grits may take an additional 20 to 30 minutes to cook. Quick grits can also be used; simply adjust your water amount and cooking time as directed on the package. Polenta and savory oatmeal are other great options, if you're wanting to switch things up a bit. And if you want to add a little extra protein goodness, you can certainly add an egg (or JUST Egg) cooked your favorite way.

Make the grits: Combine the grits, warm water, milk, and salt in a medium saucepan. Bring the grits to a boil over medium-high heat, then reduce the heat to low and simmer, stirring often, until tender, thick, and creamy with no lumps, about 20 minutes. If the grits begin to bubble and splatter or are thickening too much, add just a little hot water to the pot and give it a stir. Repeat this step, if needed.

Stir in the butter and the cheddar and stir until melted (add more cheese, if you like it cheesier). Give it a taste and add more salt, if needed.

Meanwhile, prepare the vegetables: Heat the olive oil in a large skillet over medium-high heat. Add the mushrooms and sauté until golden, 8 to 10 minutes.

Add the smoked paprika, season liberally with salt and pepper, and sauté for 1 minute. Transfer the mushrooms to a plate. Reduce the heat to medium-low and pour a little more olive oil into the pan. Add the garlic and sauté for 30 seconds, then add the spinach and sauté the spinach until wilted, 3 to 5 minutes. Season with salt and pepper. Transfer the spinach to the plate with the mushrooms.

Increase the heat under the skillet to medium, add the tomatoes, and sauté until warmed through, 2 to 3 minutes. Season with salt and pepper and transfer to the plate with the mushrooms and spinach.

Make the smoked paprika butter: Using the same skillet (no need to clean it), melt the butter over medium-low heat. Stir in the smoked paprika and a pinch of salt. Simmer for 1 minute and then remove from the heat.

Ladle the grits into two bowls and top with the mushrooms, spinach, and tomatoes. Drizzle each bowl with a little bit of the smoked paprika butter and sprinkle with a pinch of chile flakes.

GRITS

¾ cup (128 g) white or yellow grits (fine- to medium-grind)

2¾ cups (650 ml) warm water

½ cup (120 ml) whole milk

1 teaspoon fine sea salt, plus more to taste

2 tablespoons (30 g) unsalted butter

1¼ ounces (35 g) sharp cheddar cheese, coarsely grated (about ½ cup), or more if desired

VEGETABLES

2 tablespoons extra-virgin olive oil, plus more as needed

8 ounces (225 g) beech mushrooms or sliced cremini

¼ teaspoon smoked paprika

Fine sea salt and freshly ground black pepper to taste

1 garlic clove, minced

4 cups (80 g) loosely packed baby spinach

½ pint (145 g) cherry tomatoes, halved (about 1 cup)

SMOKED PAPRIKA BUTTER

3 tablespoons (45 g) unsalted butter

¼ teaspoon smoked paprika

Pinch of fine sea salt

Pinch of red chile flakes

Veganize it

Use unsweetened nondairy milk or water in place of the whole milk and nondairy butter. Omit the cheese or use meltable vegan cheese shreds.

Loaded
EGG & BEAN BURRITOS

Serves 4

BEANS

1 (15-ounce/425 g) can pinto or black beans, drained and rinsed, or 1½ cups/277 g home-cooked beans

⅛ teaspoon ground cumin

Extra-virgin olive oil

Fine sea salt and freshly ground black pepper to taste

EGG SCRAMBLE

1½ tablespoons canola oil

1 small bell pepper (either red or green or half of each), finely diced

¼ medium yellow onion, finely diced

Fine sea salt and freshly ground black pepper to taste

3 large eggs

4 (10-inch/25 cm) burrito-size flour tortillas

Cooking oil spray

2½ ounces (70 g) sharp cheddar or Monterey Jack cheese, coarsely grated (about 1 cup)

FOR SERVING

Salsa

Chunky Guacamole (page 166)

Sour cream

These small burritos are fun to make and easily adaptable. For this, I use pinto or black beans, a simple egg scramble, and cheese. All that deliciousness is wrapped into a burrito-size flour tortilla, and the filling options are endless. Keep in mind that these are also great for days when you need breakfast to-go—your future self will thank you.

Make the beans: Combine the beans, ¼ cup (60 ml) water, the cumin, and a drizzle of olive oil in a small saucepan. Season with salt and pepper. Simmer over medium-low heat for 5 minutes, until the beans are warmed through and the flavors have melded. Use a potato masher to smash the beans to your desired consistency. If the beans look dry, add water 1 tablespoon at a time to smooth them out.

Make the egg scramble: Heat the canola oil in a large nonstick skillet over medium-low heat. Add the bell pepper and onion and sauté until softened, about 5 minutes. Season lightly with salt and pepper and push the mixture to one side of the skillet. Whisk the eggs and a pinch each of salt and pepper in a small bowl. Pour the mixture into the empty side of the skillet and scramble the eggs using a silicone spatula; once scrambled, incorporate the bell pepper and onion mixture with the eggs. Transfer the scramble to a bowl and, off the heat, carefully wipe the skillet clean.

On a cutting board, spread 1 flour tortilla with one-quarter of the beans. Add one-quarter of the egg scramble, and 4 tablespoons of the cheese. Fold each side slightly toward the center. Turn and then fold the other sides toward the center to enclose the mixture. Place seam side down on a plate. Repeat with the remaining tortillas, beans, egg scramble, and cheese. (They do not have to be perfect.)

Set the same skillet over medium heat and mist the skillet with cooking spray. Place 2 burritos, seam side down, into the skillet and mist the tops lightly with the cooking spray. Cook until golden and crispy, 3 to 4 minutes, then carefully flip to the other side and cook until golden and crispy, a couple more minutes. Transfer the cooked burritos to a plate and repeat this step with the remaining burritos. Put 1 burrito on each of 4 plates and serve with salsa, guacamole, and sour cream.

Freestyle it

Other additions to consider: avocado, egg whites (in place of the whole eggs), feta cheese, hash browns, kale, mushrooms, roasted potatoes or sweet potatoes, soy chorizo, spinach, sun-dried tomatoes

Veganize it

Use a tofu scramble or JUST Egg as an egg replacement. Omit the cheese or use meltable vegan cheese shreds.

Smoked Trout & Asparagus
FRITTATA

Serves 6 to 8

There are frittatas, and then there is *this* frittata. The harmonious combination of smoked trout and asparagus is a crowd-pleaser and will have everyone saying, "Oh wow!" with the first bite. After trying it, my friend Yolanda recommended topping each slice with a dollop of either sour cream or crème fraîche. It's an elegant touch and adds a bright note. Pair this with the Parmesan, Arugula & Pear Salad (page 38).

Arrange an oven rack in the top one-third of the oven and preheat the oven to 350°F (180°C). Lightly grease a 9-inch (23 cm) or 10-inch (25 cm) pie pan with olive oil and set aside.

Heat the 1 tablespoon olive oil in a large skillet over medium-low heat. Add the asparagus and sauté until slightly softened, 3 to 5 minutes. Season lightly with salt and pepper.

Whisk the eggs in a medium bowl along with the milk, chives, dill, ½ teaspoon fine sea salt, and ¼ teaspoon ground black pepper. Add half of the cheddar and fold it in with a silicone spatula.

Layer the asparagus in the bottom of the prepared pan. Pour the egg mixture over the asparagus. Sprinkle with the rest of the cheese and the smoked trout. Transfer to the oven and bake until the center is no longer jiggly and the top is slightly golden in spots, 25 to 35 minutes, if using a 10-inch pie pan and 30 to 40 minutes, if using a 9-inch pie pan.

Allow to cool for 5 to 10 minutes before slicing. Serve slices topped with a dollop of sour cream or crème fraîche and some fresh dill (if you're being a little fancy).

Olive oil for the pie pan

1 tablespoon extra-virgin olive oil

12 ounces (340 g) asparagus, trimmed and cut on a diagonal into ½-inch (1.3 cm) pieces

Fine sea salt and ground black pepper to taste

10 large eggs

⅓ cup (80 ml) whole milk

1 tablespoon minced fresh chives

2 teaspoons minced fresh dill, plus more for serving

2½ ounces (70 g) sharp white cheddar cheese, coarsely grated (about 1 cup)

4 ounces (115 g) smoked trout, flaked

Sour cream or crème fraîche, for serving

Freestyle it

Substitutions for asparagus or smoked trout: baby broccoli, broccoli, broccoli rabe, fiddleheads, garlic scapes, kale, mushrooms, peas, smoked salmon, spinach, squash blossoms, Swiss chard

Substitutions for white cheddar cheese: feta, fontina, goat cheese, Gruyère, Swiss cheese

Substitutions for dill or chives: basil, cilantro, oregano, parsley, scallions

Bowls
OF GOODNESS

Building bowls has always been a way for me to get creative with the things I have in the pantry and the odds and ends that I have in the crisper. When building a bowl, I usually have a theme in mind and I try to select ingredients or toppings that complement each other. My bowls typically start with a base of grains (see Cooking Grains, pages 178–179) or sometimes even plain yogurt, cottage cheese, pureed vegetables, noodles, or pasta. And then I top that with a combination of some of my favorite things: raw, pickled, or cooked vegetables or fruit; prepared salads; proteins such as beans, legumes, seafood, eggs, tempeh, or tofu; and nuts, seeds, cheese, microgreens, or fresh herbs. And then I usually include a sauce or condiment to tie everything together.

DIY SPICY TOFU *Bowls*

Serves 2 (with leftovers)

CHIPOTLE SAUCE

1 canned chipotle pepper in adobo sauce plus 1 to 2 tablespoons adobo sauce (depending on your spice tolerance)

1 tablespoon fresh lime juice

2 tablespoons tomato paste

½ teaspoon dried oregano

½ teaspoon garlic powder

¼ teaspoon ground coriander

¼ teaspoon ground cumin

TOFU

2 tablespoons canola oil

1 (14-ounce/397 g) package extra-firm tofu, drained and pressed (see How to Press Tofu, page 18)

Fine sea salt

1 tablespoon fresh lime juice

FOR ASSEMBLY

2 cups (320 g) cooked Long-Grain White Rice or other cooked grain (see Cooking Grains, page 178)

Pico de Gallo (page 133) or salsa

Sour cream

Chunky Guacamole (recipe follows)

Shredded cheese

Shredded lettuce

Pinto beans (canned or A Big Ol' Pot of Beans, page 208) or black beans

Corn kernels, fresh, thawed frozen, or canned

Freestyle it

Substitutions for tofu: cauliflower, seitan, tempeh

Other ideas to consider: Instead of a bowl, use the tofu mixture as a filling in burritos, tacos, or quesadillas or on top of nachos.

This bowl was inspired by one of my favorite bowls sold at a popular Mexican-inspired restaurant chain, but it's so much better! I created this recipe when most of the city was locked down during the pandemic. What I love about this bowl is that it can be as much or as minimal as you'd like, and the toppings are really up to you. When building the bowls, set up a small toppings bar. That way each person can add whatever toppings they like. See the Michelle's Tip on page 88 for how to save any leftover chipotle peppers so you can use them in other recipes, such as my Vegetable & Black Bean Tortilla Soup (page 88).

Make the chipotle sauce: Combine the chipotle pepper, 1 tablespoon adobo sauce (or 2, if you'd like it spicier), ⅓ cup (80 ml) water, the lime juice, tomato paste, oregano, garlic powder, coriander, and cumin in a small food processor or high-powered blender. Process until smooth and set the chipotle sauce aside.

Prepare the tofu: Heat the canola oil in a large nonstick or cast-iron skillet over medium-high heat. Crumble the tofu into the skillet and cook, stirring occasionally and breaking up any large pieces with the tip of a silicone spatula, until the tofu starts to look golden and slightly crispy, similar to scrambled eggs, 11 to 13 minutes. Season lightly with salt and continue to brown the tofu, 1 to 2 more minutes.

Stir the chipotle sauce into the skillet with the tofu and mix well. Reduce the heat to low and cook, stirring occasionally, until most of the moisture has cooked off, 8 to 10 more minutes. Stir in the lime juice, give it a taste, and add more salt, if needed.

Assemble the bowls: Add rice to each of two bowls. Top with some of the tofu and any desired toppings.

CHUNKY GUACAMOLE

Makes about 1¾ cups (400 g)

2 medium avocados, halved and pitted

Small handful of roughly chopped fresh cilantro leaves

1 small jalapeño, seeded and finely diced

1 medium Roma tomato, seeded and roughly chopped

1 tablespoon fresh lime juice

Fine sea salt and freshly ground black pepper to taste

Scoop the avocado flesh into a small bowl and mash with a fork until slightly chunky. Add the cilantro, jalapeño, tomato, and lime juice. Season with salt and pepper and stir to combine.

Veganize it

For the toppings, use vegan sour cream and vegan cheese shreds.

The "I Love You" BOWL

Serves 4

The last time I was at Aviva by Kameel café in Atlanta, the owner, Kameel, walked along the customer line and gave samples to all of his hungry patrons. And as he did so, he said, "I love you" to each person. I hope he still does this. It is by far one of the sweetest gestures I've ever seen from a restaurant owner—and the food there is pretty amazing too. This vibrant bowl is inspired by Kameel. I Love You. (Smile.) For this, I roast cauliflower and golden beets in a flavorful shawarma-inspired blend of spices and then drizzle them with my favorite herby green tahini sauce. Yes, I realize that this bowl has several different components, but it's so worth it. For any leftover roasted cauliflower or beets, stuff them into a wrap or pita bread with other accompaniments.

Make Ahead

Make the green tahini sauce and refrigerate until serving.

Roast the cauliflower and beets: Preheat the oven to 400°F (200°C).

Combine the cauliflower, beets, and a good drizzle of olive oil in a large bowl (one that won't stain from the beets).

Combine the garlic powder, cumin, coriander, paprika, salt, black pepper, cinnamon, and cayenne (if using) in a small bowl and thoroughly mix. Sprinkle in the spice blend over the cauliflower and beets and toss together, ensuring that everything is evenly coated.

Transfer the mixture to a sheet pan (or two, if needed) and roast until the cauliflower is slightly golden and the beets are fork-tender, 25 to 30 minutes. Give it a taste and add more salt, if needed.

Make the salad: Combine the cucumber, tomatoes, red onion, parsley, lemon juice, and a drizzle of olive oil in a medium bowl. Season with salt and pepper and toss together. Cover and refrigerate until ready to serve.

Assemble the bowls: Divide the couscous among each of 4 bowls with the cauliflower and beets, the salad, and a good drizzle of the green tahini sauce. Serve with desired toppings.

Green Tahini Sauce (recipe follows)

SPICED CAULIFLOWER AND BEETS

1 large head cauliflower, cut into bite-size florets

3 medium golden or red beets, ends trimmed and diced into ¾-inch (2 cm) pieces

Extra-virgin olive oil

1 teaspoon garlic powder

1 teaspoon ground cumin

1 teaspoon ground coriander

1 teaspoon paprika

1 teaspoon fine sea salt, or to taste

¼ teaspoon ground black pepper

⅛ teaspoon ground cinnamon

⅛ teaspoon cayenne pepper (optional)

SALAD

½ medium English cucumber, finely diced (about 1 cup/130 g)

1 cup (180 g) finely diced tomatoes

¼ cup (30 g) finely diced red onion

¼ cup (10 g) loosely packed flat-leaf parsley leaves, roughly chopped

1 tablespoon fresh lemon juice

Extra-virgin olive oil

Fine sea salt and freshly ground black pepper to taste

FOR ASSEMBLY

4 cups (628 g) cooked couscous or other cooked grain (see Cooking Grains, page 178)

Chopped fresh mint leaves or flat-leaf parsley leaves (optional)

Quick-Pickled Red Onions (page 199) (optional)

My Favorite Hummus (page 147) or store-bought (optional)

RECIPE CONTINUES →

GREEN TAHINI SAUCE

Makes about 1 cup (240 ml)

This sauce is great served with roasted vegetables, salads, grain bowls, baked tofu, baked potatoes, seafood, and wraps.

¼ cup (60 ml) plus 2 tablespoons well-stirred tahini

½ cup (15 g) loosely packed cilantro leaves and tender stems (or a combination of other fresh herbs such as chives, basil, parsley, mint, or dill)

1 garlic clove, smashed

2 to 3 tablespoons fresh lemon juice

1 teaspoon pure maple syrup

Fine sea salt to taste

Combine ½ cup (120 ml) water, the tahini, cilantro, garlic, lemon juice (start with 2 tablespoons), maple syrup, and salt in a small food processor or high-powered blender. Blend until smooth. Taste and add the remaining 1 tablespoon lemon juice and more salt, if desired. If the sauce is too thick, add water a tablespoon at a time to thin to the desired consistency. Store it in an airtight container and refrigerate. It will keep for up to 4 days.

SHRIMP WITH VEGETABLES
Bowls

Serves 2 (with leftovers)

This recipe reminds me of a time when I was visiting my family in Cleveland and my sisters and I decided to have a girls' night and grab dinner at Benihana. My nephew, who was young at the time, loved Benihana and when he heard that we were going, he threw the biggest fit because he wanted to go too. Needless to say, we made sure to bring home food for him. Though this dish is not exactly like the offerings at Benihana, I think of him whenever I make it. I enjoy serving this with my Spicy Mayo Sauce . . . which is great for drizzling or dipping (or both!) the shrimp and vegetables.

Make Ahead Make the spicy mayo sauce as directed and refrigerate until serving.

Prepare the shrimp and vegetables: Place the shrimp in a medium bowl and season lightly with salt and pepper.

Heat the canola oil in a large nonstick or cast-iron skillet over medium-high heat. Add the zucchini and onion and cook undisturbed until golden on one side, about 3 minutes. Stir and sauté until the onion has softened and the zucchini is cooked but still a bit firm, 2 to 3 more minutes. Transfer the vegetables to a bowl, cover, and set aside.

Using the same skillet, heat a little more canola oil, if needed, over medium heat. Add the shrimp and cook on one side until pink and slightly golden on the bottom, 3 to 4 minutes. Flip the shrimp and cook on the other side until pink and opaque, 1 to 2 more minutes. Add the butter and once melted, add the garlic and the tamari and sauté until fragrant, about 30 seconds. Squeeze the lemon juice over the shrimp and season with more salt and pepper, if needed.

Assemble the bowls: Add the brown rice to each of two bowls. Top with some of the shrimp and vegetables. Drizzle with the spicy mayo sauce or serve the sauce on the side (there may be some left over). Shower with scallions and sesame seeds and live your best life.

Spicy Mayo Sauce (recipe follows)

SHRIMP AND VEGETABLES

1 pound (450 g) large shrimp, peeled and deveined

Fine sea salt and freshly ground black pepper to taste

1 tablespoon canola oil, plus more as needed

1 medium to large zucchini, thinly sliced

1 large yellow onion, thinly sliced

1 tablespoon (15 g) unsalted butter

1 garlic clove, minced

1 tablespoon tamari or soy sauce

½ medium lemon

FOR ASSEMBLY

2 cups (404 g) cooked Brown Rice or other cooked grain (see Cooking Grains, page 178)

Sliced scallions

Toasted sesame seeds

Freestyle it

Other additions to consider: bell peppers, bok choy, broccoli, carrots, mushrooms, napa cabbage, sugar snap peas, snow peas

Veganize it

Omit the shrimp and consider adding smoked tofu. Veganize the Spicy Mayo Sauce (recipe follows).

RECIPE CONTINUES →

SPICY MAYO SAUCE

Makes about ⅔ cup (145 g)

½ cup (112 g) mayonnaise
1 tablespoon Sriracha sauce, or more to taste
1 tablespoon tamari or soy sauce
1 tablespoon toasted sesame oil

Whisk together 1 tablespoon water, the mayonnaise, Sriracha, tamari, and sesame oil in a small bowl. Give it a taste and add more Sriracha, if you prefer it to be a little spicier. Add a little more water, if you prefer a thinner sauce. Transfer the spicy mayo sauce to a small airtight container and refrigerate until ready to serve or for up to 5 days.

Veganize it

Use vegan mayonnaise.

Grilled MAHIMAHI
with Mango Salsa Bowls

Serves 2

ALEX'S FAVORITE SPICE BLEND

2 teaspoons smoked paprika

1 teaspoon dried oregano

1 teaspoon fine sea salt, or to taste

1 teaspoon garlic powder

½ teaspoon onion powder

½ teaspoon ground black pepper

¼ teaspoon cayenne pepper

¼ teaspoon ground cumin

MANGO SALSA

1 medium mango, roughly chopped (about 1 cup/165 g)

1 medium tomato, seeded and roughly chopped (about ½ cup/90 g)

1 small jalapeño, seeded and minced

¼ cup (32 g) finely diced red onion

1 tablespoon fresh lime juice

¼ cup (10 g) loosely packed fresh cilantro leaves, roughly chopped

Fine sea salt and freshly ground black pepper to taste

MAHIMAHI

2 mahimahi fillets (6 ounces/170 g) each

Extra-virgin olive oil, for grilling

Canola oil, for stovetop cooking

FOR ASSEMBLY

2 cups (320 g) Coconut Jasmine Rice or other cooked grain (see Cooking Grains, page 178)

⅔ cup cooked black beans

1 lime, cut into wedges

Cilantro leaves

This is one of Alex's favorite recipes, mainly because he loves the spice blend (which has a little heat to it) I use to season the mahimahi, and I agree. It's a good one. I use mahimahi here, but it goes well on grouper, halibut, salmon, scallops, shrimp, vegetables—you get the idea. I typically serve this with my Coconut Jasmine Rice (page 178) along with some black beans and warm tortillas. And if mangoes are not in season, check below for other ways to freestyle it.

Make Ahead **Make the spice blend:** Combine the smoked paprika, oregano, salt, garlic powder, onion powder, black pepper, cayenne, and cumin in a small bowl and mix well. Set aside until ready to use and store any leftover spice blend in a small airtight container for up to 6 months.

Make Ahead **Make the mango salsa:** Combine the mango, tomato, jalapeño, red onion, lime juice, and cilantro in a small bowl. Season with salt and pepper and mix together. Cover and refrigerate for 30 minutes to allow the flavors to marry.

Cook the mahimahi: You can either grill the fish or cook it in a skillet.

To grill: Heat an outdoor grill to 400°F (200°C) or to medium heat.

Put the mahimahi fillets on a plate and pat dry with a paper towel. Drizzle both sides with a little olive oil and season liberally with the spice blend. Grill on each side for 5 to 7 minutes, depending on the thickness of the fish and the temperature of the grill. The fillets should be slightly golden and flake easily. Remove the fillets from the grill and transfer to a plate.

To cook indoors: Heat 1 tablespoon canola oil in a large nonstick or cast-iron skillet over medium heat. Cook the mahimahi until golden in color and the fish easily flakes with a fork, 5 to 7 minutes per side, depending on the thickness of the fish.

Assemble the bowls: Add some coconut jasmine rice to each of two bowls. Top each with a mahimahi fillet (I like to break my fillet into chunks), black beans, and mango salsa. Squeeze with a lime half and garnish with a little cilantro.

Freestyle it

Substitutions for mahimahi: grouper, halibut, red snapper, rockfish, salmon, scallops, sea bass, shrimp on skewers

Substitutions for mango: peaches, pineapples, strawberries

Veganize it

Use grilled or roasted cauliflower steaks, smoked tofu, or veggie kebabs.

Spicy Tuna
BOWLS

Serves 2 (with leftovers)

This bowl is basically deconstructed tuna sushi, and it's for days when I crave sushi but don't have fresh tuna on hand. I make this canned tuna version for lunch *a lot* during the week. And when I'm looking for something a little lighter, I substitute romaine lettuce for the rice. Other options: If you have leftover brown or white rice, use that instead of sushi rice and just drizzle the reheated rice with a little seasoned rice vinegar. Or you can do a crispy rice situation: Drizzle a little neutral oil in a large skillet, mash the rice down, and fry until golden and crispy.

Make Ahead

Make the spicy tuna: Combine the tuna, mayonnaise, Sriracha, sesame oil, and tamari in a medium bowl and mix well. Cover and refrigerate until you're ready to make the bowls.

Assemble the bowls: Place the frozen edamame in a small bowl of hot water. Let them thaw for several minutes and then drain.

Add some sushi rice to each of two bowls. Top with some of the spicy tuna mixture along with the edamame, cucumber, and carrot. Serve garnished with nori (if using), sesame seeds, and scallions.

SPICY TUNA

2 (5-ounce/142 g) cans water-packed wild-caught chunk light tuna, drained

¼ cup (55 g) plus 1 tablespoon mayonnaise, Hellmann's or Kewpie (Japanese mayonnaise)

1 tablespoon Sriracha sauce

1 teaspoon toasted sesame oil

1 teaspoon tamari or soy sauce, plus more for serving

FOR ASSEMBLY

½ cup (80 g) frozen shelled edamame

2 cups (367 g) cooked sushi rice or other cooked grain (see Cooking Grains, page 178)

½ medium English cucumber, halved lengthwise and thinly sliced (about 1 cup/133 g)

1 medium carrot, shredded or cut into 1-inch (2.5 cm) matchsticks (about ½ cup/110 g)

Nori snack sheets (optional)

Black or toasted white sesame seeds

Sliced scallions

Freestyle it

Substitutions for tuna: canned boneless or baked salmon, imitation crabmeat, cooked and roughly chopped shrimp

Other additions to consider: avocado, furikake seasoning, vegan kimchi

Veganize it

Omit the tuna and use grilled, baked, or fried tofu as a topping. Use vegan mayonnaise to make Spicy Mayo Sauce (page 173) to drizzle on top.

Cooking Grains

What would a Bowls of Goodness chapter be without including how to prepare some of my favorite grains and pasta (I'm looking at you, couscous!)? Optionally you could use riced cauliflower or even riced broccoli for a more plant-forward approach.

Basmati Rice

Makes about 3 cups (400 g)

1 cup (200 g) basmati rice, rinsed until water runs clear
½ teaspoon fine sea salt

Bring 1¾ cups (415 ml) water to a boil in a medium saucepan over medium heat. Stir in the basmati rice and salt. Partially cover the saucepan (to allow some steam to escape) or use a vented lid and reduce the heat to low. Simmer the rice until all of the water is absorbed, 18 to 20 minutes. Remove the saucepan from the heat and let it rest, covered, about 5 minutes. Uncover and lightly fluff the rice with a fork and serve.

Brown Rice

Makes about 2¼ cups (450 g)

1 cup (180 g) brown rice, rinsed until water runs clear
½ teaspoon fine sea salt

Fill a medium saucepan with water and bring to a boil over medium heat. Add the brown rice and salt and simmer until the brown rice is tender, 25 to 30 minutes. Drain in a fine-mesh sieve, return to the saucepan, and cover. Let the brown rice rest for about 5 minutes. Uncover and lightly fluff the rice with a fork and serve.

Coconut Jasmine Rice

Makes about 3 cups (480 g)

1 cup (240 ml) canned lite coconut milk
1 cup (185 g) jasmine rice, rinsed until water runs clear
2 teaspoons pure cane sugar or granulated sugar
¼ teaspoon fine sea salt

Bring ¾ cup (175 ml) water and the coconut milk to a boil in a medium saucepan over medium heat. Stir in the jasmine rice, sugar, and salt. Partially cover the saucepan (to allow some steam to escape) or use a vented lid and reduce the heat to low. Simmer the rice until all of the coconut milk and water is absorbed, 15 to 18 minutes. Remove the saucepan from the heat and let it rest, covered, for 5 minutes. Uncover and lightly fluff the rice with a fork and serve.

Michelle's Tip

To make cilantro-lime rice, stir in 1 to 2 tablespoons fresh lime juice and a small handful of roughly chopped cilantro leaves.

Couscous

Makes 2 to 2½ cups (314 to 393 g)

2¼ cups (530 ml) vegetable broth or water
1 cup (195 g) couscous
Extra-virgin olive oil
½ teaspoon fine sea salt

Bring the vegetable broth to a boil in a medium saucepan over medium heat. Add the couscous, drizzle with a little olive oil, sprinkle in the salt, and stir. Cover the saucepan and remove from the heat. Let it rest, covered, until all of the broth has been absorbed, about 5 minutes. Uncover and lightly fluff the couscous with a fork and serve.

Pearled Barley

Makes about 3 cups (470 g)

1 cup (200 g) pearled barley, rinsed
½ teaspoon fine sea salt

Fill a medium saucepan with water and bring to a boil over medium heat. Add the pearled barley and salt and simmer until the barley is tender but not mushy, 25 to 30 minutes. Drain in a fine-mesh sieve, return to the saucepan, and cover. Let the pearled barley rest for 5 minutes and serve.

Pearled Couscous

Makes about 3 cups (485 g)

1 cup (150 g) pearled couscous
½ teaspoon fine sea salt

Fill a medium saucepan with water and bring to a boil over medium heat. Stir in the pearled couscous and salt and simmer until the pearled couscous is tender, 8 to 10 minutes. Drain in a fine-mesh sieve and serve.

Pearled Farro

Makes about 3 cups (440 g)

1 cup (200 g) pearled farro, rinsed
½ teaspoon fine sea salt

Fill a medium saucepan with water and bring to a boil over medium heat. Add the pearled farro and salt and simmer until the farro is tender but not mushy, 15 to 20 minutes. Drain in a fine-mesh sieve, return to the saucepan, and cover. Let the pearled farro rest for 5 minutes and serve.

Quinoa

Makes about 2¼ cups (415 g)

¾ cup (130 g) quinoa, rinsed
½ teaspoon fine sea salt

Bring 1½ cups (360 ml) water to a boil in a medium saucepan over medium heat. Stir in the quinoa and salt. Partially cover the saucepan (to allow some steam to escape) or use a vented lid and reduce the heat to medium-low. Simmer the quinoa until all of the water is absorbed, about 15 minutes. Remove the saucepan from the heat and let it rest, covered, for 5 minutes. Uncover and lightly fluff the quinoa with a fork and serve.

Sushi Rice

Makes about 3 cups (550 g)

1 cup (200 g) sushi or short-grain rice, rinsed until water runs clear
¼ cup (60 ml) unseasoned rice vinegar
2 tablespoons pure cane sugar or granulated sugar
½ teaspoon fine sea salt

Bring 1½ cups (360 ml) water to a boil in a medium saucepan over medium heat (for firmer rice, use 1¼ cups/300 ml water). Stir in the rice. Partially cover the saucepan (to allow some steam to escape) or use a vented lid and reduce the heat to low. Simmer the rice until all of the water is absorbed, 18 to 20 minutes. Remove the saucepan from the heat and let it rest, covered, for 5 minutes.

Uncover and lightly fluff the rice with a fork, then transfer to a large bowl. Mix the unseasoned rice vinegar, sugar, and salt in a small bowl until the sugar and salt are completely dissolved. Once dissolved, drizzle the mixture evenly over the rice and give the rice a stir. Allow time for the rice to cool and then serve.

Long-Grain White Rice

Makes about 3 cups (480 g)

1 cup (185 g) long-grain white rice, rinsed until water runs clear
½ teaspoon fine sea salt

Bring 2 cups (473 ml) water to a boil in a medium saucepan over medium heat. Stir in the long-grain rice and salt. Partially cover the saucepan (to allow some steam to escape) or use a vented lid and reduce the heat to low. Simmer the rice, until all of the water is absorbed, about 15 minutes. Remove the saucepan from the heat and let it rest, covered, about 5 minutes. Uncover and lightly fluff the rice with a fork and serve.

SUBSTANTIAL

Sides

This chapter is all about side dishes, which have always been my favorite parts of every meal. Even as a child, if you gave me a vegetable plate, I was a happy camper. The more options, the better. But, not too long ago, I was speaking to my Auntie Gayle, who told me that she doesn't eat many vegetables. Well, that kind of surprised me, so I asked her, "What do you eat then?" She went on to say that there weren't a lot of vegetables that she liked and the ones that she did eat typically didn't have a lot of flavor. That made me realize that this is likely the case for a lot of people, which inspired me to want to change that with more substantial and flavorful side dishes.

Maple-Glazed
CARROT MEDALLIONS

Serves 4

2 pounds (910 g) rainbow carrots, if available, trimmed, peeled, and cut on a diagonal into ½-inch (1.3 cm) pieces

3 tablespoons extra-virgin olive oil

1½ teaspoons garam masala

1 teaspoon fine sea salt, or to taste

1 to 2 tablespoons pure maple syrup, to taste

These carrots will turn carrot haters into lovers with just one bite. Every time I pull them from the oven, most of them don't even make it to the platter because I literally just stand in the kitchen eating them. I season these with garam masala, which is a flavorful spice blend from India. Though rainbow carrots make for a lovely presentation, regular carrots work just as well. These are also great over a smear of garlic labneh or even a whipped feta mixture topped with some fresh herbs.

Preheat the oven to 425°F (220°C). Place a sheet pan in the oven while it preheats.

Combine the carrots, olive oil, garam masala, and salt in a large bowl and toss. Once the oven is preheated, remove the sheet pan and carefully arrange the carrots on it in one layer. Roast until the carrots are fork-tender and slightly golden, 20 to 25 minutes, giving the carrots a toss halfway through cooking.

Drizzle the maple syrup over the roasted carrots, toss them lightly, and let sit for 2 minutes before serving. (If you desire slightly sweeter carrots, add 1 more tablespoon of maple syrup.) Transfer the carrots to a serving platter (if they make it that far!) and serve.

Roasted CAULIFLOWER
with Lemon Butter Caper Sauce

Serves 4

This bright lemony dish is not only a fabulous side but it's also wonderful served over a light pasta like angel hair or orzo. Think the flavors of shrimp scampi . . . but with a vegetarian flair. Pair it with a small green salad and some warm artisanal bread to soak up all of that lemony butter sauce.

Preheat the oven to 450°F (230°C). Place a sheet pan in the oven while it preheats.

Combine the cauliflower and a good drizzle of olive oil in a large bowl. Season with salt and pepper and toss to thoroughly coat.

Once the oven is preheated, remove the sheet pan and carefully arrange the cauliflower on the pan in one layer. Roast until the cauliflower is golden and fork-tender, 20 to 25 minutes, giving the cauliflower a toss halfway through cooking.

When the cauliflower has about 5 more minutes to cook, melt the butter in a medium skillet over medium heat. Add the garlic, capers, Italian seasoning, and chile flakes. Sauté until the garlic is fragrant, about 1 minute. Stir in the lemon zest and juice. (Goodness, I love that smell!) Give it a taste and season with salt and pepper, if needed.

Transfer the cauliflower to a serving platter and pour the sauce on top. Lightly toss to coat and top with parmesan and parsley.

1 medium to large head cauliflower, cut into bite-size florets

Extra-virgin olive oil

Fine sea salt and freshly ground black pepper to taste

6 tablespoons (90 g) unsalted butter

3 garlic cloves, minced

2 tablespoons nonpareil capers, drained

½ teaspoon Italian seasoning

Pinch of red chile flakes

1 teaspoon grated lemon zest

2 tablespoons fresh lemon juice

Freshly shredded parmesan cheese, for garnish

Chopped fresh flat-leaf parsley leaves, for garnish

Veganize it

Use nondairy butter and vegan parmesan cheese.

Michelle's Tip

To easily peel and mince a garlic clove: Lay the wide end of your chef's knife blade flat over the garlic clove. Use your other hand to gently hit down on the blade. The peels from the garlic should then easily release from the clove. To mince the garlic clove: Lay the knife blade flat over the clove and press firmly down on the knife using your other hand, smashing the clove. Then use your knife to finely chop or mince the garlic.

Summer SQUASH
with Spicy Crema

Serves 2 to 4

SPICY CREMA

½ cup (115 g) sour cream or plain yogurt

1 teaspoon crushed Calabrian chile peppers in oil, or more if desired

1 small garlic clove, finely grated

Fine sea salt to taste

SUMMER SQUASH

3 to 4 small zucchini and/or small yellow squash (4 to 6 inches/10 to 15 cm long)

Fine sea salt

1 tablespoon extra-virgin olive oil

Freshly ground black pepper

Honey or hot honey

FOR SERVING

Chopped dill leaves, cilantro leaves, or flat-leaf parsley leaves

Feta cheese

Although this is great any time of the year, I highly suggest making it when zucchini and yellow squash are in season, especially for those of you who have gardens and grow your own or those of you who have access to farmers' markets. A few things to note about the zucchini and yellow squash: If you can only find medium to large zucchini or squash, you may only need two. And if they are thick, cut them in thirds lengthwise and then into shorter lengths if necessary, so that they can fit into your skillet. The crosshatch marks make for a pretty presentation, but it's not a must for this recipe. The important part is getting a nice sear on each side. As for the spicy crema, it's the perfect accompaniment and I use it with so many different grilled or roasted veggies. I find crushed Calabrian chile peppers at places like Trader Joe's, Whole Foods, or online. Harissa is a good substitute. And if you don't feel like turning on the stove, then grilling the squash is also another good option.

Make Ahead **Make the spicy crema:** Combine the sour cream, Calabrian chile peppers, and garlic in a small bowl. Season with salt and mix well. Transfer the crema to an airtight container and store in the refrigerator until ready to serve or for up to 4 days.

Prepare the summer squash: Trim the ends of the squash, halved them lengthwise, and then cut the flesh side with crosshatch marks (see photograph). Place the cut summer squash on a plate or cutting board and lightly season with salt. Let it sit for about 15 minutes to draw out some of the moisture, then lightly pat dry.

Heat the olive oil in a large skillet over medium-high heat. Working in batches if necessary, add the squash halves cut side down, without crowding the pan. Sear until the squash is golden, 5 to 7 minutes. Flip and cook until golden on the second side, 2 to 3 minutes. Transfer to a plate and season lightly with salt and pepper and add a good drizzle of honey.

To serve: Smear the spicy crema onto a large platter and arrange the squash on top. Garnish with the dill and feta cheese and serve. (How delicious does that look?!)

Veganize it

Omit the honey or use a little bit of agave nectar or pure maple syrup instead. And use vegan sour cream or nondairy plain yogurt and vegan feta cheese.

Parmesan
SUMMER CORN

Serves 6

My only experience eating creamed corn when I was younger was the kind that came from the can, and I was *not* a fan. When I began to experiment with this dish as an adult, my whole idea of what creamed corn should taste like changed: a sweet but savory taste of summer in each and every bite. There is just nothing quite like it. The trick to making this creamy is blending a bit of the corn with the heavy cream.

Combine ½ cup (120 ml) water, ½ cup (90 g) of the corn kernels, and the heavy cream in a small food processor or high-powered blender and process until smooth. Set the blended corn mixture aside.

Melt 2 tablespoons (30 g) of the butter in a large nonstick or cast-iron skillet over medium heat. Add the onion and sauté until softened, about 5 minutes. Add the remaining 5½ heaping cups (840 g) corn kernels to the skillet and sauté until the corn has softened, 5 to 8 minutes.

Reduce the heat to medium-low and stir in the blended corn mixture, the remaining 2 tablespoons (30 g) butter, and the parmesan. Simmer for another 5 minutes. If the corn is too "soupy," let it simmer a little longer to thicken. Taste, season with salt and pepper, and serve.

6 heaping cups (930 g) fresh corn kernels (from about 6 ears)

½ cup (120 ml) heavy cream, plus more as needed

4 tablespoons (60 g) unsalted butter

½ medium yellow onion, finely diced

1½ ounces (42 g) parmesan cheese, freshly grated (about ½ cup), plus more as desired

Fine sea salt and freshly ground black pepper to taste

Veganize it

Use unsweetened nondairy creamer for the heavy cream, nondairy butter, and vegan parmesan cheese.

Roasted BABY BROCCOLI
with Romesco Sauce

Serves 2 to 4

¼ cup Romesco Sauce (recipe follows)

1 pound (450 g) baby broccoli, hard ends trimmed and thick stalks halved lengthwise

Extra-virgin olive oil

Fine sea salt and freshly ground black pepper to taste

Pinch of red chile flakes

Crumbled feta cheese

This may very well be one of my favorite ways to enjoy baby broccoli. Served over romesco sauce . . . it's like a match made in food heaven. But here's the thing about baby broccoli stalks: They're not all the same thickness. So, if you're only able to find thinner baby broccoli, they will likely cook faster than the thicker kind. Do yourself a favor and serve this with some fresh crusty bread to assist in eating up any extra romesco sauce. And slather any leftover romesco sauce on sandwiches, serve with eggs or roasted vegetables, or toss with pasta.

Make Ahead Make the romesco sauce as directed and refrigerate until serving.

Preheat the oven to 400°F (200°C).

Arrange the baby broccoli in one layer on a large sheet pan. Generously drizzle with olive oil and season liberally with salt and pepper. Toss to thoroughly coat the baby broccoli. Transfer the sheet pan to the oven and roast until just fork-tender, 10 to 15 minutes (thinner stalks will cook in 10 minutes; thicker stalks will cook in 15 minutes).

Spread the romesco sauce on a platter and arrange the roasted baby broccoli on top. Top with the chile flakes, a drizzle of olive oil, and some feta cheese.

ROMESCO SAUCE

Makes about 1½ cups (410 g)

1 (12-ounce/355 ml) jar roasted red bell peppers, drained

2 garlic cloves, smashed

1 tablespoon roughly chopped drained oil-packed sun-dried tomatoes

1 tablespoon red wine vinegar or fresh lemon juice

1 tablespoon extra-virgin olive oil (alternatively, you can use the oil from the sun-dried tomatoes)

¼ cup (24 g) sliced almonds, raw or toasted (see Michelle's Tip, page 38)

¼ cup (10 g) loosely packed fresh flat-leaf parsley leaves (optional)

Pinch of red chile flakes

¼ teaspoon smoked paprika

Fine sea salt and freshly ground black pepper to taste

Combine the roasted red bell pepper, garlic, sun-dried tomatoes, vinegar, olive oil, almonds, parsley, chile flakes, and smoked paprika in a food processor or high-powered blender. Season with salt and pepper and blend the romesco sauce to your desired consistency, either slightly chunky or completely smooth. Give it a taste and add more salt, if needed. Transfer the sauce to an airtight container and store in the refrigerator until ready to serve or for up to 4 days.

Freestyle it

Substitutions for roasted baby broccoli: roasted asparagus, broccoli, Brussels sprouts, cabbage, cauliflower, potatoes, Romanesco; grilled or pan-seared eggplant, squash, or zucchini

Other ideas to consider: serve butter beans, corona beans, or pan-seared gnocchi over the romesco sauce drizzled with a little olive oil and fresh herbs.

Veganize it

Omit the feta cheese or use vegan feta cheese.

Smokin' BRAISED COLLARD GREENS

Serves 6 to 8

When I changed my dietary lifestyle, I had to figure out a new way to cook collard greens. Mom and I always cooked them with ham hocks or smoked turkey, when I was younger. I needed to create that smoky taste without the meat. So, for that, I rely heavily on smoked paprika and liquid smoke to bring out those flavors along with a little bit of garlic. Be sure to taste and salt your broth to find a nice balance between that and the tamari, because I don't want you to end up with a bland pot of greens. For a little kick, I also occasionally add a few dashes of hot sauce or pepper sauce. If you have any collard greens left, make a collard green melt sandwich like Turkey and the Wolf serves in New Orleans, or do like Chef Todd Richards, restauranteur and author of *Soul*, and add them to a bowl of your favorite vegetable ramen noodles for a different twist.

Heat the olive oil in a large pot or Dutch oven over medium-low heat. Add the onion and sauté until softened, about 5 minutes. Add the garlic, chile flakes, and smoked paprika and sauté until fragrant, about 1 minute. Stir in the vegetable broth, fire-roasted tomatoes, tamari, garlic powder, liquid smoke, black pepper, and salt.

Bring to a boil over medium heat, then add several handfuls of collard greens at a time, stirring to help wilt them and incorporate them into the broth. Once they have wilted down, add several more handfuls until all of the collard greens are in the pot. Cover tightly and simmer over medium-low heat, stirring occasionally, for 30 minutes. Taste the broth (or "potlikker" as we call it) and add tamari or salt, if needed. Continue simmering until the collard greens are tender, 10 to 15 minutes. If at any point the level of broth gets too low, add more vegetable broth, ½ cup (120 ml) at a time, to the pot. Remove from the heat and serve.

3 tablespoons extra-virgin olive oil

1 small yellow onion, thinly sliced

4 garlic cloves, minced

¼ teaspoon red chile flakes

1 tablespoon smoked paprika

3 cups (710 ml) vegetable broth, store-bought or homemade (page 68), plus more as needed

1 (14.5-ounce/411 g) can diced fire-roasted tomatoes, drained well

1 tablespoon tamari

½ teaspoon garlic powder

½ teaspoon liquid smoke

¼ teaspoon ground black pepper

Fine sea salt to taste

3 pounds (1.4 kg) collard greens, thick stems removed (see Michelle's Tip), leaves halved and cut into strips ½ inch (1.3 cm) wide

Freestyle it

Substitutions for collard greens: kale, mustard greens, turnip greens, or a mixture of different greens

Michelle's Tip

To easily destem collard green leaves, hold the stem of a collard green leaf in one hand. Using the other hand, place your index finger and thumb around the base of the stem and run those fingers along the line of the stem and midrib. Gently pull the leaf portion away from the stem and midrib. This technique also works great for kale and Swiss chard.

Grilled CORN
with Chimichurri Sauce

Chimichurri Sauce (recipe follows)

6 ears fresh yellow corn, unhusked

Kosher salt and freshly ground black pepper to taste

I am unapologetically a stan of fresh corn. And when it's in season, I throw some on the grill every chance I get. So, for this recipe I recommend using a grill to cook fresh corn in one of two ways: You can either steam the ears in their husks or remove the husks and wrap each ear in foil. By steaming them, you lock in the moisture and you're left with juicy and crisp kernels. Alternatively, if you don't want to use the grill, you can boil them in a large pot of salted water for about 5 minutes. Grilled corn is just the beginning of the wonderful world of all the things that you can enliven with this chimichurri sauce. Get inspired and create a whole platter of veggies or grilled seafood and top it with this sauce!

Make Ahead Make the chimichurri sauce as directed and refrigerate if making well ahead.

To prepare the corn in husks: Gather a large pot or bowl and fill with enough water to cover the corn. Soak for at least 30 to 60 minutes. Drain and set aside until ready to grill.

To prepare the corn in foil: Remove the husks and silk, then rinse. Tear off 6 pieces of foil, each 8 to 10 inches (20 to 25 cm) long, and individually wrap each ear of corn. Set aside until ready to grill.

Heat an outdoor grill to 375°F (190°C) to 400°F (200°C) or medium-high heat.

Grill the corn until the corn is bright yellow and cooked entirely through, 15 to 20 minutes, using a pair of tongs to turn the ears every 3 to 5 minutes. When cooking the corn with the husks on, they will char slightly on the outside; this is okay. If it looks like the husks are charring or cooking too fast, then place them on a higher rack or move to a place on the grill that is not directly over the flames.

To check to see if the corn is done, carefully pull back one of the husks or peek into the foil. If uncertain, take a small knife and cut a few kernels off one of the ends and taste them. If the corn is not done, press the husks or foil back in place and cook for an additional 3 to 5 minutes and repeat this step. There may be some charred spots on the corn and that is okay.

Transfer the corn to a sheet pan to cool for a few minutes. Once cool enough to handle, pull the husks back and remove and compost or discard any silk. If using foil, carefully remove the corn from each wrapper. Transfer the corn to a serving platter, season with kosher salt and pepper, if desired, and drizzle liberally with the chimichurri sauce (there may be some leftover). Serve immediately.

RECIPE CONTINUES →

CHIMICHURRI SAUCE

Makes about ⅔ cup (160 g)

The first time I tried chimichurri sauce was years ago at an Argentinean restaurant in Atlanta. It was served as an accompaniment to the empanadas I had ordered, and I've been making it at home ever since. I like to use cilantro, but you can also use parsley or basil, if you prefer.

1 cup (30 g) loosely packed fresh cilantro leaves, finely chopped
½ cup (120 ml) extra-virgin olive oil
1 tablespoon red wine vinegar
3 garlic cloves, finely grated
½ teaspoon dried oregano
½ teaspoon fine sea salt, or to taste
¼ teaspoon red chile flakes (optional)
¼ teaspoon ground black pepper

Combine the cilantro, olive oil, vinegar, garlic, oregano, salt, chile flakes, and black pepper in a small bowl, and mix them together. Give it a taste and adjust the seasoning, if needed. Cover and set aside for 30 minutes to allow the flavors to marry. The chimichurri sauce can be made up to 5 days ahead, stored in an airtight container, and refrigerated. The oil will solidify once refrigerated. Let it sit at room temperature for 15 to 30 minutes to allow the oil to liquefy before using.

SMASHED POTATOES

Serves 4

These loaded Mediterranean-inspired smashed potatoes are a real crowd-pleaser—they will be devoured *quickly*—and they're great as a side dish or an appetizer. Yes, there are several moving parts to this, but they are so worth it! If pressed for time, French fries, tater puffs, and even toasted pita chips (if serving immediately) are some other fun alternatives for the base.

Make Ahead Quick-pickle the red onions as directed and refrigerate until serving. Make the tzatziki sauce as directed and refrigerate until serving.

Cook the potatoes: Preheat the oven to 450°F (230°C).

Put the potatoes in a large pot and add water to cover the potatoes by several inches. Bring to a boil over medium heat, then continue to boil until the largest potato is fork-tender, 15 to 25 minutes. Drain and, once cool enough to handle, place the potatoes evenly spaced on a large sheet pan.

Using the bottom of a large glass, gently press down on each potato until ¼ inch (6 mm) thick. They don't have to be perfect. Drizzle with the olive oil, sprinkle with the oregano, and season liberally with salt. Transfer to the oven and bake until they are golden and slightly crispy, 20 to 25 minutes, flipping halfway through. Squeeze the lemon over the roasted potatoes when they come out of the oven.

To serve: Transfer the potatoes to a serving platter, top with the tomato, olives, pepperoncini, feta, tzatziki sauce, pickled red onions, and dill. Serve immediately. (Goodness that looks good!)

Quick-Pickled Red Onions (recipe follows)

Tzatziki Sauce (recipe follows)

POTATOES

1½ pounds (680 g) petite gold potatoes

3 tablespoons extra-virgin olive oil

1 teaspoon dried oregano

Fine sea salt

½ medium lemon

FOR SERVING

1 medium tomato, seeded and roughly chopped

½ cup (80 g) pitted kalamata olives, halved

6 pepperoncini peppers, stemmed, seeded, and thinly sliced

2 ounces (56 g) feta cheese, crumbled (about ½ cup)

Flaky sea salt (optional)

Chopped fresh dill

Freestyle it

Other ideas to consider:

Make parmesan smashed potatoes: Sprinkle parmesan cheese liberally onto the baked smashed potatoes and place them under the broiler for 1 to 2 minutes until golden and melted, then top with fresh parsley.

Make Buffalo smashed potatoes: Add several dashes of Frank's RedHot Buffalo Wings hot sauce onto the baked smashed potatoes along with crumbled blue cheese, thinly sliced celery, and thinly sliced scallions or chives; serve with blue cheese or ranch dressing on the side.

Veganize it

Omit the feta cheese or use vegan feta cheese when serving.

RECIPE CONTINUES ⟶

QUICK-PICKLED RED ONIONS

Makes about 1½ cups (165 g)

I love putting these on tacos, sandwiches, salads, grain bowls, and basically any dish that I want to enliven with a zingy and colorful pop of flavor. Other things I enjoy adding in to enhance the flavor are a thinly sliced clove of garlic, sprigs of dill, a bay leaf, black peppercorns, mustard seeds, or red chile flakes.

¾ cup (175 ml) unseasoned rice vinegar
¼ cup (60 ml) apple cider vinegar
1 tablespoon pure cane sugar or granulated sugar
1 teaspoon fine sea salt
1 medium red onion, halved and thinly sliced

Combine both vinegars, the sugar, and salt in a small saucepan over low heat. Gently warm until the sugar and salt are completely dissolved in the vinegar, then remove from the heat. Cool slightly. Put the red onion into a mason jar or other heatproof glass container with an airtight lid. Pour the vinegar mixture over the red onion to cover. Put on the lid slightly ajar until cooled completely. Seal and store in the refrigerator for at least 2 hours to allow the flavors to marry, the longer the better. These will keep in the refrigerator for up to 2 weeks.

TZATZIKI SAUCE

Makes about ⅔ cup (170 g)

3 inches (7.5 cm) of a medium English cucumber
½ cup (115 g) plain whole-milk Greek yogurt or sour cream
1 small garlic clove, finely grated
1 teaspoon red wine vinegar or distilled white vinegar
1 teaspoon extra-virgin olive oil
Fine sea salt and freshly ground black pepper to taste

Halve the cucumber lengthwise and seed. Grate on the medium holes of a box grater. Squeeze out the excess water from the cucumber and place in a small bowl. Add the yogurt, garlic, vinegar, and olive oil. Season with salt and pepper and mix well. The tzatziki sauce can be made up to 3 days ahead, and kept refrigerated in an airtight container.

Veganize it

Use nondairy yogurt or vegan sour cream in the tzatziki sauce.

Simple
ZINGY GREEN BEANS

Serves 2 to 4

Fine sea salt

1 pound (450 g) haricots verts or young green beans, trimmed or untrimmed

2 tablespoons extra-virgin olive oil

Freshly ground black pepper

1 small shallot, finely diced (about ¼ cup/35 g)

1 tablespoon (15 g) unsalted butter

2 garlic cloves, minced

1 tablespoon tamari or soy sauce, plus more to taste

1 tablespoon fresh lemon juice, plus more to taste

Pinch of red chile flakes (optional)

When I was younger, I typically prepared green beans by simmering them until they were extremely tender, usually with a few potatoes thrown in the pot to make them a little heartier. I still love that way of preparing them, but I find that sautéing them is equally delicious. This is a simple dish, jazzed up with fresh lemon juice and just a touch of tamari to add a little depth of flavor—and shallots, which bring just a touch of sweetness.

Blanch the green beans: Bring a large pot of salted water to a boil over medium-high heat and add the green beans. Once the water returns to a boil, blanch the green beans for 1 minute, then drain. Set aside.

Sauté the green beans: Heat the olive oil in a large nonstick or cast-iron skillet over medium-high heat. Add the green beans to the skillet and sauté, stirring every few minutes, until they begin to shrivel and slightly char in some spots, 7 to 9 minutes.

Season lightly with salt (but not too much . . . because you'll be adding tamari as well) and pepper, add the shallot, and sauté until softened, 2 to 3 minutes. Reduce the heat to medium-low. Add the butter, garlic, tamari, lemon juice, and chile flakes (if using) and sauté until the butter is melted and the sauce is incorporated with the green bean mixture, 1 to 2 more minutes. Give it a taste and add more salt, tamari, or lemon juice, if needed, then serve.

Freestyle it

Substitutions for haricots verts:
long beans, Romano beans, yellow wax beans

Veganize it

Use nondairy butter.

Roasted BRUSSELS SPROUTS

with Sweet Chili Aioli

Serves 4

I think we all have vegetables that we hated when we were kids but love as adults. Brussels sprouts are on that small list for me. Today they are a beloved vegetable and roasting them makes all the difference in their flavor. They start to caramelize slightly and the leaves get nice and crispy. I pair them with a sweet chili aioli inspired by bang bang sauce, which adds another level of flavor to basically any roasted vegetable. It's a little bit sweet, spicy, savory . . . and it is so good!

Make Ahead
Make the sweet chili aioli sauce: Mix the mayonnaise, sweet chili sauce, tamari, and Sriracha in a small bowl. Transfer the sauce to an airtight container and store in the refrigerator until ready to serve or for up to 4 days.

Roast the Brussels sprouts: Preheat the oven to 425°F (220°C).

Combine the Brussels sprouts, olive oil, garlic powder, and chile flakes (if using) in a large bowl. Season liberally with salt and pepper and lightly toss to evenly coat. Transfer to a large sheet pan and arrange in one layer, cut sides down. Transfer to the oven and roast until deep golden in color (or slightly charred in some spots, if desired), 20 to 25 minutes.

Transfer the roasted Brussels sprouts to a platter and serve the sweet chili aioli on the side for dipping.

SWEET CHILI AIOLI SAUCE

½ cup (112 g) mayonnaise

2 tablespoons Thai sweet chili sauce

1 tablespoon tamari or soy sauce

1 tablespoon Sriracha sauce

BRUSSELS SPROUTS

2 pounds (910 g) Brussels sprouts, trimmed and halved

3 tablespoons extra-virgin olive oil

½ teaspoon garlic powder

Pinch of red chile flakes (optional)

Fine sea salt and freshly ground black pepper to taste

Veganize it
Use vegan mayonnaise.

Roasted SWEET POTATOES

with Orange Miso Tahini Sauce

Serves 4

ORANGE MISO TAHINI SAUCE

¼ cup (60 ml) well-stirred tahini

¼ cup (60 ml) orange juice, freshly squeezed or store-bought, plus more as needed

1½ tablespoons pure maple syrup

1½ teaspoons white miso

½ teaspoon toasted sesame oil

Fine sea salt to taste

SWEET POTATOES

2 pounds (910 g) sweet potatoes, halved lengthwise and cut crosswise into half-moons ½ inch (1.3 cm) thick

3 tablespoons extra-virgin olive oil

½ teaspoon garlic powder

Fine sea salt and freshly ground black pepper to taste

FOR SERVING

Sesame seeds, toasted (see Michelle's Tip)

Sliced scallions

Chopped fresh flat-leaf parsley leaves or cilantro leaves

This flavorful combination has that whole sweet and savory thing going on with tender yet crispy sweet potatoes and the citrusy umami flavor of the orange miso tahini sauce. The sauce is so scrumptious, you will immediately start thinking of the many ways you can use it.

Make Ahead Make the orange miso tahini sauce: Whisk together the tahini, orange juice, maple syrup, miso, and sesame oil in a small bowl. Taste and add salt, if needed. If the sauce seems too thick, add just a touch more orange juice. This sauce can be made up to 24 hours ahead and will keep in the refrigerator, stored in an airtight container, for up to 4 days.

Roast the sweet potatoes: Preheat the oven to 425°F (220°C). Line a sheet pan with parchment paper.

Combine the sweet potatoes, olive oil, and garlic powder in a large bowl. Season with salt and pepper and toss together. Arrange in one layer on the prepared pan.

Transfer to the oven and roast until fork-tender and slightly crispy on the edges, 25 to 35 minutes, flipping the potatoes halfway through. Once done, cool slightly, 2 to 3 minutes.

Transfer the sweet potatoes to a serving platter and drizzle generously with the orange miso tahini sauce and shower with sesame seeds, scallions, and parsley.

Michelle's Tip

To toast sesame seeds, put them in a skillet over medium-low heat and toast them, stirring often, until slightly golden, 5 to 10 minutes, and then remove from the skillet.

Freestyle it

Substitutions for roasted sweet potatoes: roasted beets, broccoli, Brussels sprouts, cabbage, carrots, cauliflower, delicata squash, Honeynut squash, Japanese eggplant, Japanese sweet potatoes, kabocha squash, parsnips

Substitutions for sesame seeds: roughly chopped roasted cashews or peanuts

Mashed POTATOES
with Marsala-Mushroom Gravy

Serves 4

This dish is comfort food at its finest! It was very close to being in the Bowls of Goodness chapter because I could literally just have this as a meal and call it a day, but I digress. I believe what really sets these mashed potatoes apart from others you may have had is definitely the gravy. Everyone will taste the love that you put into it. Use this gravy anywhere you normally would—over rice, biscuits, dressing, stuffing, or pureed/mashed cauliflower.

Make the mashed potatoes: Put the potatoes in medium saucepan with water to cover by several inches. Bring to a boil over medium heat and cook until the potatoes are fork-tender, 15 to 20 minutes. Drain the potatoes and return them to the saucepan.

Use a potato masher to thoroughly mash the potatoes. Add the milk, sour cream, butter, and mayonnaise (if using). Season with salt and pepper. Mash again until all the ingredients are fully incorporated and you have a smooth, creamy consistency. Add a little more milk if the consistency is too thick. Taste and add more butter, salt, or pepper, if needed, and cover the pot to keep warm.

Make the Marsala-mushroom gravy: Heat the canola oil in a large nonstick or cast-iron skillet over medium heat. Add the mushrooms and sauté until softened, about 5 minutes. Stir in the shallot and continue to sauté until most of the moisture from the mushrooms has cooked off and they have started to turn golden, 5 to 7 minutes. Season with salt and pepper. Add the garlic and Italian seasoning and sauté until fragrant, about 1 more minute.

Stir in the Marsala and let the wine cook off, 2 to 3 minutes. Add the butter and let it melt. Sprinkle the flour evenly on top of the mushrooms. Stir until fully incorporated and slightly golden, 1 to 2 minutes. Stir in the vegetable broth and simmer over medium-low heat for 2 to 3 minutes. Once the gravy begins to thicken, reduce the heat to low. Add the heavy cream, stirring to incorporate, and simmer for 2 to 3 more minutes to let the flavors meld. If the gravy gets too thick, stir in more vegetable broth, ½ cup (120 ml) at a time, to thin out. Give it a taste and season with salt and pepper.

Spoon the mashed potatoes onto a plate and ladle the Marsala mushroom gravy on top. Garnish with fresh parsley (if using). Pour the remaining gravy in a gravy boat to pass around at the table, if anyone wants more.

MASHED POTATOES

3 pounds (1.4 kg) russet potatoes, peeled and roughly chopped

½ cup (120 ml) whole milk, plus more as needed

¼ cup (50 g) sour cream

3 tablespoons (45 g) unsalted butter

1 tablespoon mayonnaise (optional)

Fine sea salt and freshly ground black pepper to taste

MARSALA-MUSHROOM GRAVY

2 tablespoons canola oil

1 pound (450 g) cremini mushrooms, quartered

1 small shallot, finely diced

Fine sea salt and freshly ground black pepper to taste

2 garlic cloves, minced

½ teaspoon Italian seasoning

¼ cup (60 ml) Marsala or Madeira

1 tablespoon (15 g) unsalted butter

1½ tablespoons all-purpose flour

1¼ cups (300 ml) vegetable broth, store-bought or homemade (page 68), plus more as needed

½ cup (120 ml) heavy cream

Chopped fresh flat-leaf parsley leaves (optional), for garnish

Veganize it

Use unsweetened nondairy milk, vegan sour cream, nondairy butter, vegan mayonnaise, vegan wine or vegetable broth, and unsweetened nondairy creamer for the heavy cream.

A BIG OL'
Pot of Beans

Serves 6 to 8

1 pound (450 g) dried pinto or cranberry beans

1 tablespoon extra-virgin olive oil

1 medium yellow onion, trimmed, peeled, and halved crosswise

1 medium head garlic, top trimmed and one thin papery layer removed

8 cups (1.89 liters) warm water

1 bay leaf

1 teaspoon apple cider vinegar

¼ teaspoon liquid smoke

1 tablespoon fine sea salt, or to taste

¼ teaspoon freshly ground black pepper

Though some people might think you need to add meat for a pot of beans to be flavorful, that's certainly *not* the case. I find that simply simmering them low and slow with an onion, some garlic, and a few spices really goes a long way. Here I use pinto or cranberry beans, but this recipe works just as well on other beans such as lima beans, butter beans, or black beans. Simply adjust the amount of water and salt accordingly. Beans are great in that they are fairly inexpensive and they can feed a lot of people. I love them served over rice with a few dashes of hot sauce, alongside my Smokin' Braised Collard Greens (page 193) and with a slice of my Buttermilk Corn Bread (page 123). If you have any leftovers, be sure to make my Loaded Egg & Bean Burritos (page 160).

Make Ahead Prepare the beans: Rinse the beans in a colander. Pick through the beans and compost or discard any that look bad or damaged. Put the beans in a large pot or Dutch oven and add water to cover by 2 inches (5 cm). Cover and soak them at room temperature overnight or for at least 8 hours. (Soak overnight if you plan to cook them in the morning or soak during the day if you plan to cook them in the evening.) Drain and rinse the beans and set aside. Clean the pot.

Cook the beans: Set the pot over medium heat and add the olive oil. Once shimmering, place the onion halves cut side down in the pot and slightly char or brown the onion, about 5 minutes, keeping the onion intact. Add the head of garlic cut side down and heat until fragrant, about 1 minute. Add the warm water, the soaked beans, bay leaf, vinegar, liquid smoke, salt, and black pepper. Bring to a boil over medium-high heat, cover the pot, and reduce the heat to medium-low. Simmer, stirring occasionally, until the beans are tender, 1½ to 2 hours. Be sure to taste your broth during the cook time and add more salt, if needed. If the broth level gets too low, add warm water, ½ cup (120 ml) at a time. If you prefer your beans kind of creamy, use the back of a large spoon to mash some of the beans as they are cooking. This will cloud the broth and create a creamier consistency.

Compost or discard the bay leaf and the garlic head, if you do not want to use it. If you want to use the garlic, remove the head and put it on a plate. Once cooled, squeeze the garlic cloves out onto the plate, mash them up with a fork, and stir them into the pot. Keep the onion in the pot, if desired. Give the broth a taste and add more salt, if needed, and serve.

Baked TOMATO RICE

with Castelvetrano Olives

Serves 6

This is essentially an all-in-one kind of dish where you mix everything together, throw it in the oven, and let it do its thing. Of course, I could have just as easily done this on the stove, but there's just something about the slow process of this baking in the oven that I enjoy. The house smells amazing as it cooks, and as the rice bakes it gets incredibly soft and these crispy bits form around the edges and on the bottom of the dish. So good! The green chiles in this dish add a little heat, so feel free to omit those if you prefer. Serve this with your favorite protein (baked fish, sautéed shrimp, beans, etc.) or on Taco Tuesdays with other accompaniments.

Preheat the oven to 350°F (180°C).

Melt the butter: Once the oven is heated, add the butter to a 9 × 13-inch or 2.5-quart (2.5-liter) baking dish and place on the center rack of the oven to melt the butter, being sure to keep an eye on it so it doesn't brown. It should take about 5 minutes.

Prepare the rice: Meanwhile, combine the rice, vegetable broth, scallions, bell pepper, olives, tomatoes, green chiles, salt, and black pepper in a medium bowl and mix with a silicone spatula.

Remove the baking dish from the oven and scrape the rice mixture into the dish. Stir to incorporate with the melted butter. Using oven mitts, carefully cover the baking dish tightly with aluminum foil. A tight fit is best to help lock in the moisture and steam the rice. Return the dish to the oven and bake for 1 hour, stirring halfway through and re-covering tightly. (Doesn't that smell good!)

Uncover, give it one more stir, and continue to bake, uncovered, for 5 to 10 minutes. (This bakes off any remaining moisture from the rice, if needed. If the moisture has been absorbed, go ahead and remove it from the oven.) Once done, allow to cool for 2 to 3 minutes. Fluff the rice lightly with a fork.

If desired, serve garnished with queso fresco and cilantro.

4 tablespoons (60 g) unsalted butter

1½ cups (275 g) long-grain white rice, rinsed

1 cup (240 ml) vegetable broth

6 scallions, thinly sliced

1 small red bell pepper, finely diced

½ cup (55 g) pitted Castelvetrano olives or Spanish green olives, halved

1 (14.5-ounce/411 g) ounce can petite-diced tomatoes with liquid

1 (4-ounce/113 g) can diced green chiles

1 teaspoon fine sea salt, or to taste

½ teaspoon ground black pepper

FOR SERVING (OPTIONAL)

Queso fresco or feta cheese

Chopped fresh cilantro leaves or flat-leaf parsley leaves

Freestyle it

Substitutions for scallions:
½ medium yellow or red onion or small shallot, finely diced

Substitutions for green chiles:
fresh or pickled jalapeños

Veganize it

Use nondairy butter and omit the cheese or use vegan feta cheese.

Supper
WITH LOVE

When I was growing up, Mom always referred to the last meal of the day as "dinner." And although I knew it was often used synonymously with "supper," it wasn't until I got to know Alex's grandmother that "supper" really began to stick with me. She often referred to meals that she prepared to be served later in the day as supper. Whether she was yelling "Supper's ready" to Grandpa . . . or instructing me to go and tell the boys (Alex, his uncle, and younger cousin) that supper was ready. The truth is . . . any of the meals in this book can be considered supper, or dinner for that matter, just as long as they are prepared with love.

Creamy
SPINACH & TOMATO ORZO

Serves 4

3 tablespoons (45 g) unsalted butter

½ medium yellow onion, finely diced

1 cup (168 g) orzo

3 garlic cloves, minced

½ teaspoon fine sea salt, plus more as needed

¾ cup (175 ml) half-and-half

1 ounce (28 g) parmesan cheese, freshly grated (about ⅓ cup), plus more for serving

½ pint cherry tomatoes, halved (about 1 cup/145 g)

3 cups (60 g) loosely packed baby spinach, roughly chopped

Freshly ground black pepper

Torn fresh basil leaves, for garnish

I've shared several recipes that were inspired by meals I had at restaurants that Mom and I would frequent when she was still living in the Atlanta area. And this was inspired by a dish served at one of her favorite Greek restaurants. They served the creamiest orzo with fresh, gently warmed tomatoes and just-wilted spinach with hints of garlic and fresh basil. It was so simple and divine . . . and so is this.

Melt the butter in a large deep nonstick skillet over medium-low heat. Add the onion and sauté until softened, 3 to 4 minutes. Add the orzo and garlic and sauté until the garlic is fragrant, about 1 minute. Add 2¾ cups (650 ml) water and the salt. Bring to a rapid simmer over medium heat. Reduce the heat to medium-low and simmer, stirring occasionally, until most of the water has been absorbed and the orzo is al dente, 13 to 15 minutes. Reduce the heat to low. Add the half-and-half and parmesan and stir until the cheese has melted.

Stir in the tomatoes and spinach. Remove from the heat and let the orzo stand for 2 to 3 minutes, so the residual heat can wilt the spinach, warm the tomatoes, and thicken the sauce slightly more. If the sauce gets too thick, add water a tablespoon at a time to thin to the desired consistency. Give it a taste and add more salt and some pepper, if needed. Serve garnished with basil and additional parmesan on the side.

Freestyle it

Other ideas to consider: in the spring, pan-seared artichokes, sautéed asparagus, or blanched peas with a touch of lemon zest; in the summer, sautéed corn, zucchini, or yellow squash; in the fall and winter, roasted butternut squash and sautéed kale or sautéed mushrooms and crispy shallots

Veganize it

Use nondairy butter, unsweetened nondairy creamer for the half-and-half, and vegan parmesan cheese.

Braised
HARISSA CHICKPEAS & EGGPLANT

Serves 4 to 6

If you need another flavorful one-pot dish to add to your weekly meal plans, this is it. Harissa, which originates from the western regions of North Africa, typically comes in three different forms: paste, powder or spice blend, and sauce. For this I use harissa paste, which is composed of dried chile peppers, lemon juice, garlic, oil, and spices. My favorite is made by New York Shuk, and I find it at places like Sprouts, Whole Foods, or online. It adds a subtle layer of heat, depth, and richness to this dish. It's warm and comforting; as the chickpeas cook they become soft and buttery and the eggplant will practically melt in your mouth. The kalamata olives add a briny burst of flavor to each bite. This is great served over your favorite grain with a dollop of yogurt and flatbread on the side; on a slice of toast with a poached or crispy fried egg; wrapped in flatbread with some pan-seared Halloumi or feta cheese sprinkled on top; or over a bed of warm polenta.

Preheat the oven to 425°F (220°C).

Heat the olive oil in a large cast-iron braiser (or an ovenproof skillet at least 2 inches/5 cm deep) with an ovenproof lid over medium heat. Add the red onion and sauté until softened, 3 to 5 minutes. Stir in the eggplant and sauté until it begins to soften, 2 to 3 minutes. If the pan gets too dry, drizzle in a little more olive oil. Add the garlic, smoked paprika, cumin, coriander, and garlic powder and sauté until fragrant, about 1 minute. Stir in the harissa paste (start small if you want less spice), 1 cup (240 ml) water, the tomatoes, chickpeas, bay leaf, olives, salt, and black pepper.

Cover the braiser with the lid (or tightly with foil), transfer to the oven, and bake until the eggplant softens entirely and melds with the tomatoes and chickpeas, 20 to 25 minutes. Remove from the heat (compost or discard the bay leaf). If the pan looks dry, add 1 or 2 tablespoons water and then stir in the lemon juice. Taste for salt and black pepper.

Garnish with parsley and a drizzle of olive oil, and serve with your favorite cooked grain (or whatever you're serving it with) and a dollop of yogurt.

3 tablespoons extra-virgin olive oil, plus more as needed

1 small red onion, finely diced

1 medium eggplant (about 1 pound/ 450 g), ends trimmed, peeled in alternating strips (like zebra stripes), and cut into ½-inch (1.3 cm) cubes

3 garlic cloves, minced

1 teaspoon smoked paprika

1 teaspoon ground cumin

1 teaspoon ground coriander

½ teaspoon garlic powder

1 to 2 tablespoons harissa paste, to taste

1 (14.5-ounce/411 g) can petite-diced tomatoes with liquid

1 (15-ounce/425 g) can chickpeas, drained and rinsed

1 bay leaf

½ cup (80 g) pitted kalamata olives

1 teaspoon fine sea salt, or to taste

¼ teaspoon ground black pepper

1 tablespoon fresh lemon juice

FOR SERVING

Chopped fresh flat-leaf parsley leaves or cilantro leaves

Extra-virgin olive oil, for drizzling

Cooked grain (see Cooking Grains, page 178)

Plain yogurt

Freestyle it

Substitutions for harissa: crushed Calabrian chili peppers in oil or tomato achaar, such as Brooklyn Delhi

Other ideas to consider: a combination similar to ratatouille using things like fennel, Japanese eggplant, red onion, red bell pepper, squash, or zucchini.

Veganize it

Omit the yogurt or use plain nondairy yogurt.

Cheesy BAKED PASTA
with Vegetables

Serves 6 to 8

Fine sea salt to taste

1 pound (450 g) pasta tubes, such as rigatoni or ziti

2 tablespoons olive oil

1 medium yellow onion, finely diced

8 ounces (225 g) cremini or white button mushrooms, roughly chopped

1 medium green bell pepper, finely diced

3 garlic cloves, minced

1 teaspoon Italian seasoning

Pinch of red chile flakes

1 (32-ounce/907 g) jar marinara sauce, such as Rao's or homemade

Freshly ground black pepper to taste

1 cup (245 g) whole-milk ricotta cheese, or more if desired

8 ounces (225 g) low-moisture mozzarella cheese, shredded

1½ ounces (42 g) parmesan cheese, freshly grated (about ½ cup), plus more for topping

Freestyle it

Substitutions for mushrooms: roasted eggplant, broccoli, grated carrots, plant-based ground beef or meatballs, or a couple handfuls of kale or spinach

Veganize it

Use vegan ricotta cheese or tofu ricotta and meltable vegan mozzarella cheese shreds.

Oh, my goodness! I would eat this just for that cheese pull! If you're looking for subtle ways to add (or, for some of you, hide) a few extra veggies to your meals, this is the dish for you. I love to use mushrooms, to give it a little more texture, and then add one or two other veggies, depending on what's in the crisper. I call for 32 ounces of marinara sauce for this recipe because 24 ounces just does not do the trick when it comes to 1 pound of pasta. Rao's is typically my go-to brand or I buy two 24-ounce jars and I refrigerate the leftover sauce to use on pizza later that week. If you don't have ricotta cheese in the fridge, cottage cheese is a good substitute. This dish is great for when you want to feed a larger group. Add a simple salad with it and some fresh baked bread or rolls and you'll be good to go!

Preheat the oven to 350°F (180°C).

Bring a large pot of salted water to a rolling boil over high heat. Cook the pasta until just al dente according to the package directions (the pasta will bake in the oven as well). Reserve ½ cup (120 ml) of the pasta water. Drain the pasta and set aside. Reserve the pot; you will use it for mixing later.

Heat the olive oil in a large nonstick skillet over medium heat. Add the onion, mushrooms, and bell pepper and sauté, stirring occasionally, until the mushrooms have cooked down and the onion and bell pepper have softened, 8 to 10 minutes.

Add the garlic, Italian seasoning, and chile flakes and sauté until fragrant, about 1 minute. Reduce the heat to low, add the marinara sauce, and season with salt and pepper. Stir and simmer for about 10 minutes, to allow the flavors to meld. Taste the sauce and add more salt and pepper, if needed.

Combine the pasta and sauce in the reserved pot and mix thoroughly. If the mixture is too dry, add some of the reserved pasta water to thin it out. Carefully pour half of this mixture into a 9 × 13-inch (23 × 33 cm) baking dish, spreading it out evenly. Place small dollops of ricotta cheese onto the pasta mixture and use the back of the spoon to spread the ricotta evenly over the pasta. (It's okay if it mixes slightly with the sauce.) Add the remaining pasta mixture over the layer of ricotta. Sprinkle the shredded mozzarella and parmesan evenly over this top layer of pasta.

Transfer the baking dish to the oven and bake until the cheese is melted, bubbling, and slightly golden, 30 to 35 minutes. Sprinkle with more parmesan and tell your friends or family that supper's ready and dig in!

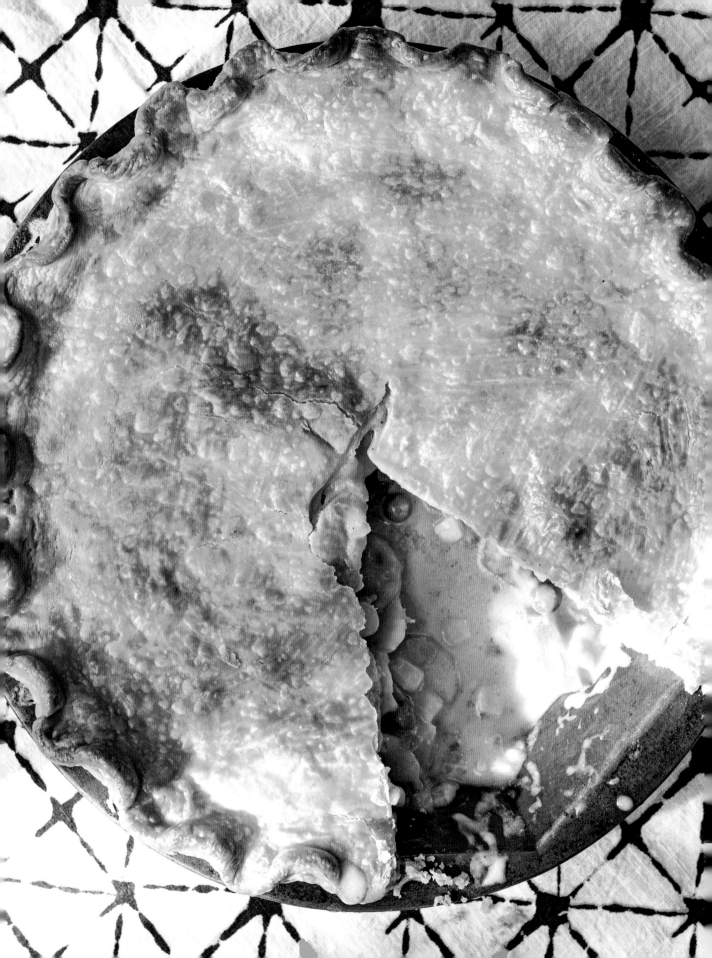

Sunday Night
VEGETABLE POT PIE

Serves 4

Sundays are typically when I'm not in a rush, and I like to make meals that take a little more time. I'll put on Etta James's "A Sunday Kind of Love," and I'll make comfort dishes like this one. Now, sometimes I do make my own pie dough, but for this recipe I take a shortcut and use store-bought. For the filling, I like to stick to 4 to 5 cups of vegetables and those can be substituted based on what you have on hand. Root vegetables take a little longer to cook, so I finely dice or thinly slice those to ensure they cook through. I also like to play around with the flavor profile by adding a small handful of chopped fresh herbs or even a little curry powder to the sauce to switch things up a bit. I encourage you to do the same.

Preheat the oven to 400°F (200°C).

Make the filling: Melt the butter in a large skillet over medium-low heat. Add the onion, potato, celery, and carrots and sauté until the potatoes and carrots have softened a bit, 10 to 15 minutes. Add the garlic and sauté until fragrant, about 1 minute. Sprinkle in the flour and stir until the flour is thoroughly incorporated and turns slightly golden, 1 to 2 minutes. The mixture will be kind of thick. Slowly stir in the vegetable broth and continue stirring until thoroughly mixed and lump-free.

Stir in the milk and simmer over low heat until the sauce is a thick gravy-like consistency, about 5 minutes. If the sauce gets too thick, add ¼ cup (60 ml) more vegetable broth and give it a stir. You want the sauce to be really creamy because the dough will absorb some of the liquid and you don't want the pot pie to be too dry. Give the sauce a taste and season it with salt and pepper. Stir in the peas, corn, and poultry seasoning (if using).

Make the pot pie: Drape one round of the pie dough evenly over a 9-inch (23 cm) pie pan and gently press to line the pan. Trim any excess dough with a knife. Pour the filling into the pan and then place the remaining round of dough over the filling. Trim any excess off and crimp the edges (as pictured or however works best for you). Cut a few slits on the top of the dough and put the pot pie on a sheet pan (just in case some of the sauce bubbles over). Put the sheet pan in the oven and bake until the top of the pot pie is golden brown and the sauce is bubbling, 25 to 35 minutes. After 15 minutes, check your pie to be sure the edge of the crust is not browning too quickly. If it is, wrap aluminum foil around the edge so that it doesn't burn. Let the pot pie cool for 5 to 10 minutes and serve.

5 tablespoons (75 g) unsalted butter

1 medium yellow onion, finely diced

1 medium russet potato, peeled and cut into ½-inch (1.3 cm) cubes

1 medium celery stalk, thinly sliced

2 medium carrots, peeled and thinly sliced

1 garlic clove, minced

¼ cup (31 g) all-purpose flour

1½ cups (360 ml) vegetable broth, store-bought or homemade (page 68), plus more as needed

1 cup (240 ml) whole milk

Fine sea salt and freshly ground black pepper to taste

¼ cup (35 g) peas, fresh or frozen

½ cup (75 g) corn kernels, fresh, frozen, or canned

⅛ teaspoon poultry seasoning (optional)

2 rounds store-bought pie dough, such as Pillsbury, thawed if frozen

Freestyle it

Substitutions for pie dough: Top the filling with drop biscuits or phyllo dough. Or make something more like a cottage or shepherd's pie using pureed celeriac, cauliflower, or mashed potatoes.

Veganize it

Use a neutral oil or nondairy butter, unsweetened nondairy milk, and vegan pie dough or puff pastry (for the top only).

Spicy LEMONGRASS TOFU
with Broccoli

Serves 4

LEMONGRASS SAUCE

1 lemongrass stalk (about 8 inches/ 20 cm long), tough outer layers peeled, halved lengthwise, and finely chopped

3 garlic cloves, peeled but whole

¼ cup (60 ml) mirin

3 tablespoons Sriracha sauce

2 tablespoons tamari or soy sauce

1 tablespoon balsamic vinegar

TOFU AND BROCCOLI

3 tablespoons canola oil

1 (14-ounce/397 g) package extra-firm tofu, drained, pressed (see How to Press Tofu, page 18), and cut into 4 thick slices (see also Michelle's Tip)

1 large broccoli crown, cut into bite-size florets (about 5 cups/450 g)

Fine sea salt

Cooked grain (see Cooking Grains, page 178) or noodles, for serving

A few years back when I was working in downtown Atlanta, there was a Vietnamese takeout restaurant that I frequented for lunch. I always ordered the spicy lemongrass tofu. When the pandemic hit and I started working remotely, I craved that spicy tofu *so* much, which inspired me to re-create it at home. The key to this recipe is getting a good fry on the tofu: Each side should be golden brown and crispy. The other is how you prepare the lemongrass to prevent your sauce from being stalky or fibrous: Peel off the tough outer layer of the lemongrass, then halve the stalk lengthwise, finely chop it, and blend it *well* in the sauce.

Make the lemongrass sauce: Put the lemongrass, garlic, mirin, Sriracha, tamari, and vinegar in a high-powered blender and blend until completely smooth, about 30 seconds. (I see you making that smooth sauce!) Set the sauce aside until ready to use.

Cook the tofu and broccoli: Heat the canola oil in a large nonstick or cast-iron skillet over medium-high heat. Tear the tofu into ¾-inch (2 cm) craggy pieces (it doesn't have to be perfect) and place evenly spaced in the skillet. Fry undisturbed, until the bottom is crispy and golden brown, 8 to 10 minutes. Flip and crisp and brown the other side, another 8 to 10 minutes. Transfer to a plate.

Compost or discard all but 1 tablespoon of oil from the pan. Add the broccoli and sauté, stirring occasionally, just until fork-tender, 5 to 8 minutes. Return the tofu to the skillet, give it a stir, and then pour in the spicy lemongrass sauce. Stir the sauce in with the tofu-broccoli mixture and cook until thoroughly incorporated, 2 to 3 more minutes. Give it a taste and season with salt, if needed.

Serve with a cooked grain or noodles.

Freestyle it

Substitutions for broccoli: asparagus, bok choy, baby broccoli, cabbage, haricots verts, sugar snap peas, snow peas

Michelle's Tip

To make the tofu slightly crispier: Toss the tofu in ⅓ cup (45 g) cornstarch or arrowroot powder and a pinch or two of salt prior to frying.

Kitchen Sink
ENCHILADA CASSEROLE

Serves 6 to 8

I make this dish *a lot* because it's just so great for using any bits and bobs that you may have in the fridge or pantry. Vegetables, grains, beans, and cheese! Oh my! Assembling this casserole is kind of like layering lasagna, so if there's anyone in the house with you, have them help out and make it a party.

Arrange an oven rack in the top one-third of the oven and preheat the oven to 375°F (190°C).

In a 9 × 13-inch (23 × 33 cm) baking dish, create the layers as follows: ¾ cup (185 g) enchilada sauce on the bottom of the dish, 5 corn tortillas over that (2 on each side and 1 in the middle), and over the tortillas the rice and black beans seasoned lightly with salt and pepper. Top the rice and beans with ½ cup (55 g) queso quesadilla. Layer over the next 5 corn tortillas (2 on each side and 1 in the middle), and spread ½ cup (125 g) enchilada sauce over the tortillas. Add the corn and diced tomatoes over the tortillas and season lightly with salt and pepper. Sprinkle with ½ cup (55 g) queso quesadilla. Layer the remaining 5 corn tortillas over the cheese and spread with the remaining enchilada sauce. Top with the remaining cheese.

Place the baking dish in the top one-third of the oven and bake until the top is melted and bubbling, 30 to 35 minutes.

Serve with cilantro, sour cream, scallions, avocado, and olives alongside. (And do the happy dance—after all this is a party!)

2 (10-ounce/283 g) cans red or green enchilada sauce (roughly 2⅓ cups)

15 (5½- to 6-inch) white or yellow corn tortillas

2 cups (320 g) cooked rice or other cooked grain (see Cooking Grains, page 178)

1 (15-ounce/425 g) can black beans or pinto beans, drained and rinsed, or 1½ cups/277 g home-cooked beans

Fine sea salt and freshly ground black pepper to taste

8 ounces (225 g) queso quesadilla or Monterey Jack cheese, shredded (about 2 cups)

1 cup (150 g) corn kernels, fresh, thawed frozen, or canned

1 (10-ounce/283 g) can diced tomatoes with green chilies, such as Ro-Tel, drained

FOR SERVING

Chopped fresh cilantro leaves

Sour cream

Sliced scallions

Diced avocado

Sliced black olives

Veganize it

Use meltable vegan cheese shreds and vegan sour cream.

Salmon

with Tomatoes & Red Onions

Serves 2 (with leftovers)

MARINATED TOMATOES

1 large or 2 small vine-ripe Roma tomatoes, seeded and roughly chopped (about ¾ cup/135 g)

1 tablespoon red wine vinegar

SALMON

1 pound (450 g) skinless salmon, cut into ¾-inch (2 cm) cubes

½ teaspoon dried thyme

½ teaspoon garlic powder

Fine sea salt and freshly ground black pepper to taste

2 tablespoons canola oil

½ cup (55 g) thinly sliced red onion

1 small jalapeño, seeded and thinly sliced (optional)

FOR SERVING

Cooked grain (see Cooking Grains, page 178)

1 medium lemon, quartered

Desta Ethiopian Kitchen is a well-known restaurant right outside of Atlanta. Their food is outrageously good and when I go, I typically order their salmon tibs, which is what inspired this dish. The salmon is pan-fried until golden and crispy and the tomatoes and red onions offer warm but fresh pops of sweet acidity. There are also a few jalapeño slices floating around in there, which add a slight touch of heat. (If you don't do spicy foods, feel free to omit them.) For a nice variation, add ½ teaspoon of berbere spice when you're seasoning the salmon. Berbere is a beautiful blend of spices originating from Ethiopia and Eritrea and can be found at Sprouts, Whole Foods, or online. Pair this dish with a simple salad or your favorite cooked grain.

Marinate the tomatoes: Combine the tomatoes and vinegar in a small bowl, give it a stir, and set aside to marinate.

Cook the salmon: Combine the salmon, thyme, and garlic powder in a medium bowl and season with salt and pepper. Toss to coat the salmon.

Heat the canola oil in a large nonstick or cast-iron skillet over medium heat. Add the salmon in a single layer and cook undisturbed until the bottom is golden and crispy, 3 to 5 minutes. Flip the salmon pieces gently with a fish spatula or a pair of tongs. Scatter the red onion and jalapeño (if using) on top of the salmon and cook for 2 to 3 more minutes, without disturbing the salmon. The red onion will begin to steam and get a little softer on top of the salmon.

Add the marinated tomato mixture (including the vinegar) and gently toss with the salmon. Continue cooking just to warm the tomatoes through, about 2 more minutes. They should still be slightly firm in texture and not mushy. Give the salmon a taste and add more salt, if needed.

Spoon the salmon over a cooked grain and serve with lemon wedges to squeeze over the salmon.

Freestyle it

Substitutions for salmon:
barramundi, grouper, halibut, sea bass, trout

Veganize it

Omit the salmon and use extra-firm tofu, pan-seared until crispy.

Grilled SWORDFISH
with Peach Bruschetta

Serves 2

Atlanta is not called "Hotlanta" for nothing, and as soon as the weather warms up you will find me and Alex on the back porch listening to music with a cold beverage in one hand and a pair of tongs in the other. We love grilling! Now I realize peaches are not necessarily traditional when it comes to making bruschetta, but summer peaches taste amazing in it and pair so well with grilled fish. When picking out peaches from the market, be sure to smell them. If they don't smell sweet, they are likely not quite ripe. If peaches are not in season, simply use two tomatoes for the mixture. This is great served with some fresh crusty bread to assist in eating up any extra bruschetta—and if you have any Balsamic Glaze (page 64), add a small drizzle of that as well.

Make Ahead

Make the peach bruschetta: Make this at least 30 minutes prior to serving to allow the flavors to marry. Combine the peach, tomato, red onions, olive oil, vinegar, garlic, and basil in a small bowl. Season with salt and pepper and toss together. Give it a taste and adjust the seasoning, if needed. Store in the refrigerator in an airtight container until you're ready to use or for up to 2 days.

Grill the swordfish: Heat an outdoor grill to 400°F (200°C) or to medium-high heat.

Put the swordfish on a plate and pat dry. Drizzle both sides with a little olive oil. Season with the basil, oregano, and salt and pepper. Brush the grill with a little oil to prevent sticking. Grill for 5 to 10 minutes on each side, depending on thickness. The steaks should be slightly golden and should flake easily.

Transfer the steaks to a serving platter. Squeeze juice from the lemon halves onto each steak. Spoon the peach bruschetta over the grilled swordfish (look at that deliciousness!) and serve.

PEACH BRUSCHETTA

1 medium peach, roughly chopped

1 medium tomato, seeded and roughly chopped

¼ cup (30 g) finely diced red onions

1 tablespoon extra-virgin olive oil

1 tablespoon white balsamic vinegar

1 large garlic clove, grated

Small handful fresh basil leaves, thinly sliced

Fine sea salt and freshly ground black pepper to taste

GRILLED SWORDFISH

2 swordfish steaks (8 ounces/ 225 g each), trimmed of any hard flesh around the edges

Extra-virgin olive oil, plus more for the grill

1 teaspoon dried basil

1 teaspoon dried oregano

Fine sea salt and freshly ground black pepper to taste

1 medium lemon, halved

Freestyle it

Substitutions for swordfish: grouper, halibut, mahimahi, rockfish, salmon, snapper

Veganize it

Omit the swordfish and consider grilling cauliflower steaks.

SALMON & ZUCCHINI *Skewers*
with Zhoug

Serves 2 (with leftovers)

Zhoug (recipe follows)

1 pound (450 g) skinless salmon, cut into 1-inch (2.5 cm) cubes

2 medium zucchini (about 1 pound/ 450 g), halved lengthwise and cut crosswise into ¾-inch-thick (2 cm) half-moons

2 tablespoons extra-virgin olive oil, plus more for the grill

½ teaspoon paprika

½ teaspoon garlic powder

¼ teaspoon dried dill

Fine sea salt and freshly ground black pepper to taste

I love sauces and this fabulous Middle Eastern sauce, zhoug, is no exception. It's a little zingy and the combination of spices and herbs make it the perfect accompaniment to these skewers. Anytime they are on the menu, they are quickly devoured. What's great about these skewers is that they can be baked or grilled, so I provide instructions to do both. Pair them with a simple salad, your favorite cooked grain, and/or some flatbread or pita bread.

Make Ahead Soak six 12-inch (30 cm) bamboo skewers in water for about 30 minutes or use metal skewers.

Make the zhoug as directed and refrigerate until serving.

Cook the salmon: If baking, arrange an oven rack in the top one-third of the oven and preheat the oven to 425°F (220°C). Line a sheet pan with foil. If grilling, heat an outdoor grill to 400°F (200°C) or to medium-high heat.

Put the salmon and zucchini in a large bowl with the olive oil, paprika, garlic powder, and dill. Season liberally with salt and pepper and toss together to evenly coat the salmon and zucchini. Alternating zucchini and salmon, starting and ending with the zucchini, thread each skewer with about 4 pieces of zucchini and 3 pieces of salmon. (The first zucchini slice threaded on should be top side first; the last zucchini slice should be threaded on flesh side first. This will help sandwich the salmon and zucchini.)

To bake the skewers: Transfer the threaded skewers to the prepared sheet pan and space out evenly, cut sides of the zucchini facing down. Bake until the salmon and zucchini are slightly golden, 10 to 15 minutes. Set the broiler on high and broil the skewers for 1 to 2 minutes, just until the salmon and zucchini are slightly charred. Watch so they don't burn. If you'd like to brown the other side, use a pair of tongs or a fish spatula to carefully flip the skewers over and repeat this step.

To grill the skewers: Brush the grill with a little olive oil to prevent sticking. Transfer the skewers to the grill and cook on each side until the salmon is opaque and slightly golden, 6 to 8 minutes per side, depending on the temperature of the grill. The flesh will flake easily when done. Transfer the skewers to a sheet pan or plate.

Plate the skewers and spoon the zhoug sauce over them. Serve any remaining sauce alongside for anyone that would like more.

Freestyle it

Substitutions for salmon: mahimahi, sea scallops, shrimp, snapper, swordfish, or tuna; or Halloumi or paneer

Veganize it

Use baked tofu or an assortment of vegetables such as bell peppers, mushrooms, onions, and yellow squash.

ZHOUG

Makes about ¾ cup (200 g)

1 cup (30 g) loosely packed fresh cilantro leaves, finely chopped

½ cup (120 ml) extra-virgin olive oil

1 small jalapeño, seeded and finely diced

3 garlic cloves, finely grated

½ teaspoon ground coriander

½ teaspoon fine sea salt, or to taste

¼ teaspoon ground cumin

¼ teaspoon ground cardamom

2 tablespoons fresh lemon juice, or more to taste

Combine the cilantro, olive oil, jalapeño, garlic, coriander, salt, cumin, cardamom, and lemon juice in a small bowl and mix together. Give it a taste and add more lemon juice or salt, if needed. The sauce can be made up to 5 days ahead, stored in an airtight container and refrigerated. The oil will solidify once refrigerated. Let it sit at room temperature for 15 to 30 minutes to allow the oil to liquefy before using.

RESOURCES

NATIONAL FARMERS' MARKET AND CSA RESOURCES

Farmers Market Coalition
A national organization that provides resources about farmers' markets across the United States along with other helpful information.

farmersmarketcoalition.org

US Department of Agriculture
Provides resources to locate farmers' markets and CSAs across the United States.

usdalocalfoodportal.com

ATLANTA-AREA FARMERS' MARKET AND CSA RESOURCES

Some of my favorite local agricultural centers, farms, and local farmers' markets that I visit in the Atlanta area.

Atlanta Harvest
An urban farm and wellness center serving the greater Atlanta area that is committed to producing naturally grown food in the city.

atlantaharvest.com

Community Farmers' Markets
Community farmers' markets in the Atlanta area, including Decatur, East Atlanta Village, Grant Park, Oakhurst, Ponce City Market, and Virginia Highland.

cfmatl.org

East Point Farmers' Market
A local farmers' market that offers local produce and other merchandise.

downtowneastpoint.com/
eastpointfarmersmarket

Freedom Farmers' Market
A local farmers' market located at the Carter Center that is open year-round.

freedomfarmersmkt.org

Patchwork City Farms
Patchwork City Farms is an urban farm owned by Jamila Norman (aka Farmer J), located in the city of Atlanta, whose seasonal veggies are sold through local farmers' markets and online.

patchworkcityfarms.com

Sweet Auburn Curb Market
Referred to as the Curb Market, it houses local businesses, including produce, butchers, seafood, a bakery, a cooking school, and popular eateries.

municipalmarketatl.com

Truly Living Well
A natural urban agricultural center and nonprofit based in Atlanta.

trulylivingwell.com

Your Dekalb Farmers Market
This market offers a large selection of dry goods, meat, fresh seafood, produce, dairy products, beer and wine, a bakery, a deli, and an eatery.

dekalbfarmersmarket.com

POTTERS AND CERAMICISTS

I love handcrafted pottery and these are some of my favorite potters and ceramicists whose beautiful pieces grace some of the pages of this book.

Colleen Hennessey Clayworks
These handmade ceramics are inspired by growing and cooking food.

colleenhennessey.net

East Fork Pottery
This company designs, manufactures, and sells thoughtful, durable ceramic dishware in Asheville, North Carolina.

eastfork.com

Golden Ratio Clay Works
Thoughtfully designed ceramics for home; made by hand, made with heart.

goldenratioclayworks.com

Heath Ceramics
Beautiful handcrafted dinnerware, based in California.

heathceramics.com

Mack Ceramics
Bowls and/or plates by prop stylist and potter Claire Mack.

mackceramic.com

Mudbloom Pottery
Small-batch functional pottery, based in Atlanta, Georgia.

Instagram: mudbloompottery

Nocrumbsleft Pottery
Small line of hand-thrown bespoke pottery.

nocrumbsleft.store

Sarah Kersten
Fermentation jars and functional everyday pottery from a studio located in Oakland, California.

sarahkersten.com

PANTRY AND KITCHEN ITEMS

Sources for a few pantry and kitchen items mentioned throughout the book.

New York Shuk
This Brooklyn-based company specializes in handcrafted Middle Eastern pantry staples.

nyshuk.com

Brooklyn Delhi
Bridging cultures by connecting people to real Indian flavors, their products include delicious condiments and simmer sauces sold at grocery stores nationwide.

brooklyndelhi.com

Bee's Wrap
Unlike other plastic food storage alternatives, Bee's Wrap is natural and compostable.

beeswrap.com

Stasher Bags
Designs functional BPA-free products that inspire people to replace single-use plastic.

stasherbag.com

Souper Cubes
Portion-friendly stackable BPA-free freezer food trays.

soupercubes.com

INDEX

HarperCollins books may be purchased for educational, business, or sales promotional use. For information, please email the Special Markets Department at SPsales@harpercollins.com.

FIRST EDITION

Photographer: Erin Scott
Food Stylist: Lillian Kang
Food Stylist Assistant: Paige Arnett

Handsketched Seamless Patterns © Vitek Graphic via Creative Market

Library of Congress Cataloging-in-Publication Data has been applied for.

ISBN 978-0-06-325654-5

24 25 26 27 28 IMG 10 9 8 7 6 5 4 3 2 1

For Harper Design:
Senior Editor: Marta Schooler
Assistant Editor: Soyolmaa Lkhagvadorj
Assistant Editor: Jenna Lefkowitz
Director, Design: Lynne Yeamans
Managing Editor: Dori Carlson
Production Editorial Manager:
 Stacey Fischkelta
Recipe Editor: Tricia Levi
Proofreaders: Rita Madrigal and
 Sarah Scheffel
Indexer: Judy Lyon Davis

For Harvest:
Senior Editor: Stephanie Fletcher
Assistant Editor: Jacqueline Quirk
Senior Designer: Melissa Lotfy
Managing Editor: Jennifer Eck
Marketing: Amanda Livingston